Horse Trails
of Arizona

Horse Trails of Arizona

Mountain Trails and Camps

Dr. Michael C. Yager

Johnson Books
BOULDER

Published by Johnson Books, a division of Johnson Publishing Company, 1880 South 57th Court, Boulder, Colorado 80301. E-mail: books@jpcolorado.com www.johnsonbooks.com

Cover design: Debra Topping
Cover photo: Eldon Bowman, Ph.D., Flagstaff, AZ
Author photo: Natural Light Photography by Annette L. Mattox

9 8 7 6 5 4 3 2 1

Library of Congress Cataloging-in-Publication Data
Yager, Michael C.
    Horse trails of Arizona: mountain trails and camps / Michael C. Yager.
        p. cm.
    ISBN 1-55566-335-4
    1. Trail riding—Arizona—Guidebooks. 2. Trails—Arizona—Guidebooks. 3.
Packhorse camping—Arizona—Guidebooks. 4. Forest reserves—Arizona—
Guidebooks. 5. Arizona—Guidebooks. I. Title.
    SF309.256.A6Y34 2004
    798.2'3'09791—dc22   2003028266

Printed in the United States by
Johnson Printing
1880 South 57th Court
Boulder, Colorado 80301

Please note: Risk is always a factor in backcountry and high-mountain travel, especially when weather is adverse or unpredictable, and when unforeseen events or conditions create a hazardous situation. The author has done his best to provide the reader with accurate information about backcountry travel, as well as to point out some of its potential hazards. It is the responsibility of the user of this guide to learn the necessary skills for safe backcountry travel and to exercise caution in potentially hazardous areas. The author and publisher disclaim any liability for injury or other damage that occurs to anyone using this book.

Contents

Acknowledgments

To MY CHILDREN, Cristy and John, to my family, and to Sharon for, above all, their love and patience.

To Jane, for always agreeing that we needed another horse.

Thank you to Phil Arnold and Art Garrison for putting the horses back in my life.

Posthumously, to Emerson Walker, for insisting my trail riding was safer than bull riding.

To Sam, Sonny, and Chester, whose strong backs and legs and desire to "go" made my trail-riding experiences so great.

A special thank-you to the National Forest Service for up-to-date information and the patience to explain over and over, in particular, Frank Hayes and Rosalee Coca in Clifton, Arizona; Les Dufour in Douglas; and Peter Weinell at the Tonto headquarters in Phoenix.

Clapsaddle

Now Clapsaddle has horsepacked
    thousands of wilderness miles in many a state,
water from streams in a myriad of national forests,
    has washed his plate.

He's shepherded doctors and dentists
    and a posse of psychiatrists who had no clue,
10-year-old giggling girls
    and a high-ranking politician or two.

Clapsaddle has survived summer blizzards
    and bogs and spitting llamas;
Bear-spooked horses, Yukon Jack and spilled spaghetti
    have added to his dramas.

Take it from one who's been there
    preparation is the consummate guide,
so, let Doc Yager's experiences
    complement your successful ride.

Supplement this work with detailed maps
    and equine-understanding rangers,
select friendly trails that fit your mount
    and let others encounter the dangers.

So many routes and so many choices
    opportunities, the truth be told,
better saddle up now
    before the horses get too old!

Wilbur E. Flachman (aka Bufford T. Clapsaddle) is a Westminster, Colorado, magazine and newspaper publisher who has spent 35 summers riding timberline.

Introduction

HORSEBACK RIDING for many years served as a traditional mode of transportation and travel, particularly in the backcountry. What was once a necessity is now a recreational endeavor for many people. The high country of Arizona offers unlimited opportunities to enjoy horseback riding to its fullest. When I tire of the hot weather and the strains it places on horse and rider, I look to the high country, which offers dense forests, alpine peaks, rugged granite mountains, streams and lakes, and volcanic mountains and plateaus.

The state of Arizona can be divided into three general land types. The northern third features the Colorado plateau, with an escarpment having a mean elevation of 6,500 feet. The mountains here are volcanic, with summits rising to 10,000 feet or higher. Much of the land mass in this northern portion is plateau-like but frequently marked with rugged mountains, deep canyons, gorges, coulees, and gullies. A good deal of this land is forested with ponderosa pine.

The next lower geographic level is the Basin Range, incorporating approximately 68,000 square miles of land that lies below the impressive escarpment called the Mogollon Rim. This landmass is referred to as "transitional woodland" where oak and juniper prevail.

The third general land area includes the plains and deserts, and is generally lower in elevation than the trails and areas to be addressed in this book.

In researching the geography of Arizona, I came across a reference to biologist C. Hart Mirriam, who studied plant evolution and botanical retreat patterns. In 1889 he developed and published his thesis on plant life zones. The Mirriam hypothesis is that every 1,000 feet of elevation gain is roughly equivalent to traveling 500 miles north. Thus, the spruce-fir-aspen forest on the high peaks of southern Arizona is quite similar to the boreal forests of the southern Yukon.

Between 7,000 and 8,000 feet, Douglas fir dominates the forests, as it does in British Columbia. The pine forests at 5,000 to 6,000 feet are ecologically similar to the lowland forests of Montana. Below these, at 3,000 to 5,000 feet, is a conifer and oak woodland that gradually favors hardwoods at lower elevations. The oak woodland breaks into grassy savannas at the lower limits of the elevation range, and this gives way to the desert grasslands that dominate the lower slopes and support succulents and cacti.

The wildlife of the Arizona high country is as grand as its landscape. From late August through September, magnificent elk bulls are visible as they bugle and herd with the elk cows. In some areas mule deer are numerous and visible. Mountain lions and wild turkey are at home here as well.

This high country has many old abandoned mines, only some of which have been sealed or fenced and all of which are dangerous. Never enter a mine; the mine you enter could be your last.

Old cabins, ranches, petroglyphs, and other evidence of early civilization are also present in the high backcountry. Please do no harm to them so that they can be enjoyed by others.

It was not possible in these pages to include every trail suitable for riding. My intent was to feature trails that offer the greatest experience and pleasure, but that are also challenging. I have refrained from including trails that are also used by motorized vehicles, which can spook your horse.

A few of the trails in this book are segments of the Arizona Trail. When completed, the Arizona Trail will be a continuous 750-mile trail spanning the state from its southern border with Mexico to its northern border with Utah. It will pass through four of the six national parks located in Arizona, as well as through Grand Canyon National Park and the Coronado and Saguaro National Monuments.

As of this writing, in a few areas the designated Arizona Trail uses forest roads as trail segments. These trail segments are open to motorized vehicles and mountain bikers and thus are not usually listed in this book. However, the wilderness segments of the trail, which may not be used by motorized vehicles, are identified and cross-referenced to the national forest in which they are located to provide easy access to information on them.

Saddle up, go out, and have fun!

Happy Trails,
MCY

Trail Riding in the National Forests

Safety

CLIMATE IN THE HIGH COUNTRY is varied and severe, and potentially dangerous for both you and your horse. High heat and low humidity can contribute to dehydration, resulting in heat exhaustion, heat stroke, or even death. Do not assume that water will be available on the trail or at the trailhead. Terms like "spring" or "creek" in a trail's name do not imply the presence of water, and the streams mentioned in this book are only seasonal unless specified otherwise. It is essential to bring enough water for both you and your horse. And always confer with a forest ranger about water availability at the time you plan to ride.

In summer months especially, thunder and lightning storms can occur suddenly, turning you and your horse into "sitting ducks." Don't go under a tree for cover. Seek shelter for yourself and your horse under rock outcroppings and overhangs, and head down the mountain. Snow may be encountered at higher elevations, not only in the cooler months but also in the summer in the form of snowfields. Either rain or snow can transform a trail into a slippery, treacherous ride. Preparation for such circumstances is a must, as is obtaining up-to-date trail conditions from the ranger district office.

Supplies

THE FOLLOWING ARE SUGGESTIONS for equipping yourself and your horse.

- Lead rope and halter
- Helmet
- Insect repellent, both human and horse
- First-aid kit, both human and horse
- Easy boot

- Identification for you and the horse (on the horse, identify trails you expect to travel)
- Collapsible bucket for watering the horse
- Hoof pick
- Pocket knife
- Personal water and food
- Saddle and hat rain protection
- Wristwatch
- Compass or GPS device
- Bell tied to the horse's breast collar (to notify other trail users of your presence)
- Orange vest and orange highlight/tapes on horse or equipment (if riding in a hunting area during hunting season)
- Toilet paper and baby wipes
- Plastic bags
- Duct tape
- Nylon string or light rope
- Two cinches (to attach highline to trees)

Trail Etiquette

- Use common sense
- Ride on the right side of the trail
- Yield to uphill riders
- Speak to backpackers, as this can prevent your horse from spooking
- Pass other trail riders on the left, and advise them that you are passing
- Keep one to two horse lengths between horses, except when going downhill, and then maintain three horse lengths should the lead horse slip
- If first to the gate, hold the gate open for the last rider
- Avoid galloping
- Obey posted signs
- Wait until everyone is mounted before riding off
- Tie a colored ribbon as warning in the tail of a horse that kicks to notify other riders of this fact

Ghost Riding

GHOST RIDING is the art of leaving no trace of your use of the forest. You have gone back to nature, so let your camp area do the same.

- Plan and prepare.
- Camp and travel on durable surfaces. Stay on designated trails. Don't cut switchbacks.
- Pitch it in, pack it out.
- Properly dispose of what you cannot pack out.
- Leave what you find.
- Minimize the use and impact of fire. Use existing fire circles if possible. Save sod for naturalizing. Build fires away from tree scrubs and meadows. Burn only small sticks. *Make sure the fire is completely out.* Scatter the ashes and naturalize the area.
- Protect and conserve water resources, as riparian areas are very fragile. Wash away from camp and water source. Dig latrines at least 200 feet from camp trails and water sites.
- Use processed horse feed to discourage weed or exotic plant growth.
- Spread your horse's manure piles.
- Fill in and level any areas dug-up or trampled by your horse.

Your Horse's Health

Heat Stroke and Heat Exhaustion
Signs and Symptoms

- Reluctance to continue working or moving
- Weakness
- Stupor
- Restlessness or anxiety
- Lack of attention or disorientation
- Decreased urination
- Excessive sweating
- Skin hot to the touch
- Increased heart rate after rest: more than 60 beats per minute
- Increased respiration (panting): more than 40 breaths per minute
- Decreased pulse pressure
- Muscle twitching and trembling
- Stumbling

Complications
- Collapse
- Laminitis
- Electrolyte imbalance
- Renal failure
- Death

Treatment
- Dismount and unsaddle your horse.
- Move out of the sun.
- If water is available, give the horse several small drinks.
- Wet your shirt or T-shirt and sponge your horse's neck, back, chest, and sides to help facilitate body core cooling.
- Monitor vital signs. A normal heart rate is 40–60 beats per minute. A regular breathing rate is 12–16 breaths per minute. Regular rectal temperature is less than 102.5 degrees.
- When the vital signs have stabilized, begin walking the horse home, resting every 15 minutes. You may need to wait until evening when the temperature drops.
- Cooling the horse's hooves may help to prevent laminitis.
- Speak with your veterinarian after you get home.

Prevention
- Ride a conditioned horse or keep the ride short, slow, and sweet.
- Allow your horse to rest every 30 minutes.
- Water your horse every two to three hours, or more if the trail is strenuous and the weather is hot.

Snakebite
Signs and Symptoms
- Swelling on the legs or face
- Possible difficulty breathing
- Increased heart rate
- Possible bleeding from two puncture wounds

Treatment
- Stop and rest your horse.
- Cleanse the bite area with cool water and a Betadine solution.
- Do not use a tourniquet or lance the wound.

- Monitor vital signs. A normal heart rate is 40–60 beats per minute. A regular breathing rate is 12–16 breaths per minute. Regular rectal temperature is less than 102.5 degrees.
- Slowly return to your horse trailer, resting every 15 minutes. Seek immediate veterinary attention.

Insect Bites
Signs and Symptoms
- Anxiety
- Localized pain and swelling

Treatment
- Examine the suspected wound area for a retained stinger in the horse's skin, and remove the stinger, if found.
- Wash area with cool water and Betadine solution.
- Rest the horse. Then return home.

Horse-isms

I GREW UP AROUND accomplished horsemen. They had many great sayings regarding horses. I wanted to share them with you, the reader, and hope that they would not be lost in time.

- A horse has only two gaits—to the barn and from the barn.
- If you find a man who can hold a horse, sell the horse and hire the man.
- A fartin' mare will never tire, but a fartin' man is the one to hire.
- If a horse won't stand, he hasn't worked enough.
  —Chris C. Yager

- A lot of people don't talk to their horses. I talk to mine and mine listen.
- When driving horses, don't slap the horses with the lines—that's for the western movies. —Art Garrison

- If a horse is fartin'—it's startin'. —Dennis Kuehl

- One thing about a team of horses—one is willing to work and the other is willing to let him. —Jim Hemstreet

- There is nothing better for the inside of a man than the outside of a horse.
- No foot, no horse. —Anonymous

- A horse is designed for one purpose—self destruction.
  —Alan Nixon, D.V.M.

- A horse that rolls completely over is worth $50.00 more.
- Any old horse can fart in the morning, but a good horse will fart in the evening.
- What is time to a hog?
- All horses will run, some just sooner than others. —Lynn Meyer

- The best color of a horse is fat. —Ross Sparrow

- A good horse comes in any color. —Eldred Pierce

- Hitch a horse green and you won't be surprised by anything he does. —Orval Pierce

How to Use This Book

THE TRAILS PORTION of this guidebook is divided into six chapters, one for each national forest. A short introduction describes the topography and history of the area. A chapter index to the trails, grouped by ranger district, provides page numbers so you can find a particular trail easily. An address and a phone number for each ranger district allow you to write or call for up-to-date trail conditions and other information about the area in which you wish to ride.

Each trail is then described using the following categories.

Highlights. Aspects of interest on the trail, such as a place of historical note or a topographical feature.

Total Distance. The length of the trail, in miles. Most of the trails in this book are at least 3 miles long, unless they are connectors to more lengthy trails.

Location. The name of the area through which the trail passes.

Type of Trail. All the trails in the book are designated for equestrians and hikers; a few allow mountain bikers as well.

Connecting Trails. The names of the trails, if any, that connect with the subject trail, which give you opportunities to expand your ride.

Difficulty. This book focuses on trails that are horse-friendly, which does not necessarily mean that riding these trails will be a risk-free adventure. If you have experience with horses, you already know that they are unpredictable creatures. Be careful, especially on trails requiring experienced horses and riders. The trail ratings below indicate the degree of difficulty for both rider and horse:

Easy: Relatively flat; generally gradual increases and decreases in elevation; switchbacks generally not too cumbersome, sharp, or narrow.

> *Moderate:* Steeper and sharper increases and decreases in elevation than "easy" trails; possible loose stone; generally harder work for horse and rider than an "easy" trail.
>
> *Difficult:* Narrower than an "easy" or "moderate" trail, with steeper and sharper inclines and declines; some areas may require dismounting; requires an experienced rider and a horse with strong mountain trail experience.

Elevation. The lowest and highest elevations encountered on the ride. If the higher of the two elevations is listed first, the trail is generally a downhill ride; if the lower of the elevations is listed first, it is generally an uphill ride.

Best Months. The time(s) of the year most conducive to riding the trail. Keep in mind that even "year-round" trails may be closed at times in the winter because of inclement weather. Call the ranger district office before your trip to obtain up-to-date trail conditions.

Maps. The names of maps that include the area through which the trail passes. A national forest map, available at the Forest Service or ranger district office, is a recommended purchase. Delorme's *Arizona Atlas and Gazetteer* is a good source of topographic and trail maps; you may wish to make copies of these pages so you have a pocket version for the ride. U.S. Geological Survey (USGS) maps (quadrangles) provide detailed topographical information and can be obtained from the USGS. Map dealers, bookstores, and stores that sell outdoor recreation gear are also good places to acquire these maps.

Special Considerations. Notes of interest for planning your trip, such as lack of water on the trail or the need for a four-wheel-drive vehicle to access the trailhead. Also notes of caution, such as trail steepness or the presence of private property.

Trailhead. How to access the trail, with driving directions from the nearest town or city. Note that some trails have no trailheads, and some have more than one access point.

If you wish to camp with your horse, see the list of horse camps in the appendix. As with the trails, a description and directions for getting there are provided for each.

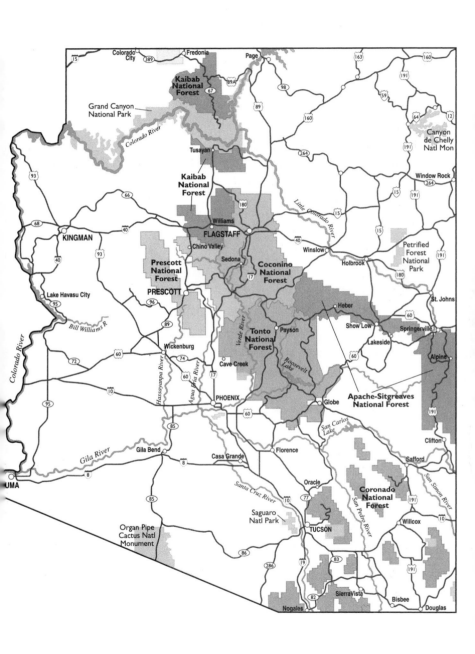

Kaibab National Forest — 67

Grand Canyon National Park

Colorado City — Fredonia — Page

Colorado River

Tusayan

Kaibab National Forest

Williams

FLAGSTAFF

Chino Valley

Sedona

Coconino National Forest

Prescott National Forest

PRESCOTT

KINGMAN

Lake Havasu City

Bill Williams R.

Colorado River

Wickenburg

Cave Creek

Tonto National Forest

Payson

Roosevelt Lake

Hassayampa River

Agua Fria River

Verde River

PHOENIX

Globe

Heber

Show Low

Lakeside

Springerville

Alpine

Apache-Sitgreaves National Forest

Winslow

Holbrook

Petrified Forest National Park

St. Johns

Clifton

Safford

Little Colorado River

Window Rock

Canyon de Chelly Natl Mon

Gila River

Gila Bend

Casa Grande

Florence

Oracle

San Carlos Lake

Santa Cruz River

Saguaro Natl Park

TUCSON

Coronado National Forest

Willcox

San Pedro River

San Simon River

Organ Pipe Cactus Natl Monument

Sierra Vista

Nogales

Bisbee

Douglas

YUMA

Apache-Sitgreaves National Forest

THE APACHE-SITGREAVES NATIONAL FOREST can truly be described as special thanks to its abundant water—more than any other national forest in the southwest. The Apache-Sitgreaves National Forest, encompassing 2.1 million acres, is home to thirty-four lakes and reservoirs and 680 miles of rivers and streams. The White Mountains, also located here, are the headwaters to the Black, the Little Colorado, and the San Francisco Rivers. Elevation ranges from 3,500 feet near Clifton to the 11,500-foot Mt. Baldy.

The Apache-Sitgreaves National Forest derives its name from the Apache Indian tribes who lived here and from Captain Lorenzo Sitgreaves, a topographical engineer who explored the area in 1850.

Apache-Sitgreaves National Forest Trails

Alpine Ranger District

Apache-Sitgreaves National Forest
Alpine Ranger District
PO Box 469
Alpine, AZ 85920
~~928-339-4384~~ 928-339-5000

Nearby City
Alpine

|

Chevelon Ranger District

Apache-Sitgreaves National Forest
Chevelon Ranger District
HC 62, Box 600
Winslow, AZ 86047
928-535-4481

Nearby Cities
Winslow, Payson, Show Low

Clifton Ranger District

Apache-Sitgreaves National Forest
Clifton Ranger District
HC 1, Box 733
Duncan, AZ 85534
928-687-1301

Nearby Cities
Clifton, Duncan

Heber Ranger District

Apache-Sitgreaves National Forest
Heber Ranger District
PO Box 968
Overgaard, AZ 85933
928-535-4481

Nearby City
Overgaard

Lakeside Ranger District

Apache-Sitgreaves National Forest
Lakeside Ranger District
RR 3, Box B-50
Pinetop-Lakeside, AZ 85929
928-368-5111

Nearby Cities
Lakeside, Pinetop, Show Low

4

Springerville Ranger District

Apache-Sitgreaves National Forest
Springerville Ranger District
PO Box 760
Springerville, AZ 85938
928-333-4372

Nearby Cities
Springerville, Eagar, Greer

San Carlos Apache Indian Reservation

To ride on the reservation, you will need a permit. Write to:

San Carlos Indian Reservation Tribal Offices
Box 0
San Carlos, AZ 85550
928-475-2343

Or, you may purchase a riding permit for $7 in the city of Globe, at the tribal office, the Apache Globe Casino, the Express Stop Store, or Circle K Store. If you ride in the Black or Salt River Recreation Area on the reservation, the permit is $20, which includes a fishing permit in that area.

Alpine Ranger District

TIGE RIM TRAIL #90

Highlights: A scenic ride.
Total Distance: 5 miles. Your ride can be lengthened via connecting trails.
Location: Blue Range Wilderness and Primitive Area
Type of Trail: Equestrian/Hiker
Connecting Trails: Bonanza Bill Trail #23
Difficulty: Easy to moderate
Elevation: 7,200 to 7,760 feet
Best Months: April through November
Maps: Apache-Sitgreaves National Forest USGS: Blue SE
Special Considerations: Side trip (a winding route through Pueblo and Tige Canyons).
Trailhead: From Alpine, drive 3 miles east on US 180 to FR 281 (Blue Ridge Road). Turn south and drive 20.7 miles to the Pueblo Park Road (FR 232). The trailhead is 4.7 miles east on this dirt road at the wooden corral.

FOOTE CREEK TRAIL #76

Highlights: Cedar Springs flows year-round.
Total Distance: 16 miles. Your ride can be lengthened via connecting trails.
Location: Blue Range Wilderness and Primitive Area
Type of Trail: Equestrian/Hiker
Connecting Trails: Grant Creek Trail #75, Horse Ridge Trail #38, Tutt Creek Trail #105
Difficulty: Difficult
Elevation: 9,200 to 5,520 feet
Best Months: May through October
Maps: Apache-Sitgreaves National Forest USGS: Hannagan Meadows, Beaver Head, Bear Mountain.
Special Considerations: Water occasionally found in Foote Creek. This trail is accessible via Horse Ridge Trail #38, and Tutt Creek Trail #105.

Trailhead: From Alpine, drive 23 miles south on US 191 to the south
end of Hannagan Meadows. Turn left (east) on FR 29A to the
Steeple/Foote Creek trailhead and parking lot. Lower access is
obtained from FR 281.

HORSE RIDGE TRAIL #38

Highlights: Great major rock formations of Castle Rock and Bell
Rock.
Total Distance: 5 miles. Your ride can be lengthened via connecting
trails.
Location: Blue Range Wilderness and Primitive Area
Type of Trail: Equestrian/Hiker
Connecting Trails: Foote Creek Trail #76
Difficulty: Moderate
Elevation: 8,100 to 6,400 feet
Best Months: May through October
Maps: Apache-Sitgreaves National Forest USGS: Beaver Head
Special Considerations: Water is occasionally found in Foote Creek.
Trailhead: Parking and trailhead are adjacent to US 191.

RASPBERRY TRAIL #35

Highlights: A pleasant equestrian trail.
Total Distance: 9.4 miles
Location: Blue Range Wilderness and Primitive Area
Type of Trail: Equestrian/Hiker
Connecting Trails: McBride Mesa Trail #26
Difficulty: Difficult
Elevation: 7,780 to 5,160 feet
Best Months: Year-round
Maps: Apache-Sitgreaves National Forest USGS: Strayhorse, Bear
Mountain
Special Considerations: This trail loops back to the Blue River Road.
Trailhead: From Alpine, drive south on US 191 32 miles to the Stray-
horse Campground. The trailhead is across from the campground.
Another trailhead is located off FR 281.

HINKLE SPRING TRAIL #30

Highlights: A canyon-to-rim trail, originally used to move cattle to and from summer range.

Total Distance: 4.5 miles. Your ride can be lengthened via connecting trails.

Location: Blue Range Wilderness and Primitive Area

Type of Trail: Equestrian/Hiker

Connecting Trails: Bonanza Bill Trail #23

Difficulty: Moderate to difficult

Elevation: 5,700 to 7,520 feet.

Best Months: May through October

Maps: Apache-Sitgreaves National Forest USGS: Blue

Special Considerations: Black bears are frequently seen in this area.

Trailhead: From Alpine, drive east of Alpine on US 180 3.5 miles to FR 281 (Blue River Road). Turn south and follow this back road 21.3 miles to the Hinkle Spring trailhead on the left.

RENO TRAIL #62

Highlights: A connecting trail to Bear Wallow Trail #63, with a steep descent into the canyon.

Total Distance: 1.9 miles. Your ride can be lengthened via connecting trails.

Location: Bear Wallow Wilderness

Type of Trail: Equestrian/Hiker

Connecting Trails: Bear Wallow Trail #63, Gobbler Point Trail #59, Rose Spring Trail #309, Schell Canyon Trail #316

Difficulty: Moderate

Elevation: 8,880 to 7,760 feet

Best Months: May through October

Maps: Apache-Sitgreaves National Forest USGS: Baldy Bill

Special Considerations: Steep switchbacks to the canyon floor. The loop between this trail and Gobbler Point Trail #59 is 7 miles long. The Reno Trail and Schell Canyon Trail are 8.3 miles in total length. You will need a permit to travel on the San Carlos Apache Indian Reservation. See page 4.

Trailhead: From Alpine, travel south on US 191 28 miles to FR 25. Head west on FR 25 5.2 miles. A pullout on the left takes you to the Reno trailhead. Parking lot is across the road from the trailhead.

SCHELL CANYON TRAIL #316

Highlights: This connecting trail has beautiful panoramic views looking south from the Colorado Plateau.

Total Distance: 2.8 miles. Your ride can be lengthened via connecting trails.

Location: Bear Wallow Wilderness

Type of Trail: Equestrian/Hiker

Connecting Trails: Rose Spring Trail #309, Bear Wallow Trail #63

Difficulty: Moderate to difficult

Elevation: 8,620 to 7,500 feet

Best Months: May through October

Maps: Apache-Sitgreaves National Forest USGS: Baldy Bill

Special Considerations: You will need a permit to travel on the San Carlos Apache Indian Reservation. See page 4.

Trailhead: From Alpine, travel south on US 191 about 29 miles to FR 54. Turn west and go 6 miles on FR 54 to a fork in the road. Stay on FR 54 about 0.6 mile farther to the end of the road. The Rose Spring Trail begins about 50 yards from here. Follow the Rose Spring Trail about 3 miles to Schell Canyon Trail #316.

ROSE SPRING TRAIL #309

Highlights: Excellent panoramic views.

Total Distance: 5.4 miles. Your ride can be lengthened via connecting trails.

Location: Bear Wallow Wilderness

Type of Trail: Equestrian/Hiker

Connecting Trails: Schell Canyon Trail #316

Difficulty: Moderate to difficult

Elevation: 8,700 to 6,700 feet

Best Months: May through October

Maps: Apache-Sitgreaves National Forest USGS: Baldy Bill

Special Considerations: You will need a permit to travel on the San Carlos Apache Indian Reservation. See page 4.

Trailhead: From Alpine, drive south on US 191 about 29 miles to FR 54. Turn west on FR 54 and travel about 6 miles to a fork in the road. The trail begins 50 yards below the parking area, which is 0.6 mile from the fork.

WS LAKE TRAIL #54

Highlights: Bear Springs offers a reliable water source. Multiple trail intersections. Great view. WS Lake is a small tank located in a 5-acre dry lakebed.

Total Distance: 11.3 miles. Your ride can be lengthened via connecting trails.

Location: Blue Range Wilderness and Primitive Area

Type of Trail: Equestrian/Hiker

Connecting Trails: Cow Flat Trail #55 at 2.8 miles, Bear Valley Trail #41 at 5.3 miles, Largo Trail #51 at 5.6 miles, Sawmill Trail #39 at 6.2 miles, side trail to Bear Mountain Lookout at 6.5 miles, terminus at Bear Springs

Difficulty: Moderate

Elevation: 8,500 to 7,460 feet

Best Months: May through October

Maps: Apache-Sitgreaves National Forest USGS: Blue, Bear Mountain

Special Considerations: No direct access. Use the Sawmill Trail #39 access to the trailhead.

Trailhead: From Alpine, drive east on US 180 3.5 miles to FR 281 (Blue River Road). Turn south and follow this road 24.5 miles to the Sawmill trailhead, on the left side of the road. Access to WS Lake Trail #54 is 5.4 miles along the Sawmill Trail.

COW FLAT TRAIL #55

Highlights: Several small waterfalls. Multiple trail intersections.

Total Distance: 12.5 miles. Your ride can be lengthened via connecting trails.

Location: Blue Range Wilderness and Primitive Area

Type of Trail: Equestrian/Hiker
Connecting Trails: South Canyon Trail #53 at 0.7 mile, Franz Spring
   Trail #53 at 1.2 miles, Lanphier Trail #52 at 1.4 miles, a shortcut to
   Franz Spring Trail #43 at 1.6 miles, WS Lake Trail #54 at 3.6 miles,
   Little Blue Trail #41 and Bear Valley Cabin at 5.2–5.3 miles, terminus
   at Blue River at 12.5 miles
Difficulty: Difficult to moderate
Elevation: 7,760 to 4,800 feet
Best Months: April through November
Maps: Apache-Sitgreaves National Forest USGS: Bear Mountain,
   Dutch Blue Alma Mesa
Special Considerations: The trail after the Cow Flat portion is marked
   with blazes and rock cairns.
Trailhead: From Alpine, drive east on US 180 3 miles to FR 281 (Blue
   River Road). Turn south, and drive 20+ miles to Pueblo Park Road
   (FR 232). Turn east and go 4.7 miles to the Bonanza Bill trailhead.

RED HILL TRAIL #56

Highlights: Good views of Castle Rock.
Total Distance: 9.7 miles. Your ride can be lengthened via connecting
   trails.
Location: Blue Range Wilderness and Primitive Area
Type of Trail: Equestrian/Hiker
Connecting Trails: Tutt Creek Trail #105
Difficulty: Difficult
Elevation: 8,000 to 5,790 feet
Best Months: May through November
Maps: Apache-Sitgreaves National Forest USGS: Beaverhead, Maness
Trailhead: From Alpine, drive south on US 191 to FR 567 (Beaverhead
   Lodge). Turn left (east) and drive about 1 mile to the signed road
   on the right leading to the trailhead.

PARADISE TRAIL #74

Highlights: A deep wilderness trail accessed only from other trails.
Total Distance: 4.2 miles. Your ride can be lengthened via connecting
   trails.

Location: Blue Range Wilderness and Primitive Area
Type of Trail: Equestrian/Hiker
Connecting Trails: Foote Creek Trail #76, Steeple Mesa Trail #73, Paradise Trail #74, Grant Creek Trail #75, Upper Grant Creek Trail #65
Difficulty: Moderate
Elevation: 7,764 to 7,360 feet
Best Months: May through October
Maps: Apache-Sitgreaves National Forest USGS: Beaverhead, Bear Mountain, Strayhorse
Trailhead: From Alpine, drive south on US 191 23.5 miles to the south end of Hannagan Meadows. Turn left (east) on FR 29A and proceed to the Steeple and Foote Creek trailhead and parking lot. Ride Foote Creek Trail #76 3.5 miles to Grant Creek Trail #75. Follow trail #75 2.4 miles to the junction with Paradise Trail #74. Approximately 2.5 miles from Steeple Mesa Trail #73, the Paradise Trail will cross Grant Greek and the junction of Upper Grant Creek Trail #65 will be available.

GRANT CREEK TRAIL #75

Highlights: A major route between the Mogollon Rim and the lush floor of Blue River Canyon.
Total Distance: 10 miles. Your ride can be lengthened via connecting trails.
Location: Blue Range Wilderness and Primitive Area
Type of Trail: Equestrian/Hiker
Connecting Trails: Grant Cabin Trail #306 at 1.5 miles, Paradise Trail #74 at 2.7 miles
Difficulty: Difficult
Elevation: 8,800 to 5,440 feet
Best Months: May through October
Maps: Apache-Sitgreaves National Forest USGS: Hannagan Meadows, Beaverhead, Bear Mountain
Special Considerations: Flowing water sources include White Oak Springs and Grant Creek.
Trailhead: From Alpine, drive south on US 191 23 miles to the south end of Hannagan Meadows. Turn left (east) on FR 29A to the

Steeple/Foote Creek trailhead and parking lot. Access Grant Creek
Trail #75 via Foote Creek Trail #76 to Bar Lake. Or, from Alpine,
travel east on US 180 3 miles to FR 281 (Blue River Road). Turn
south and follow this back road 26.5 miles to the Blue River Road
trailhead to access the Grant Creek Trail.

UPPER GRANT CREEK TRAIL #65

Highlights: Multiple trail junctions, which can provide a lengthy and
scenically varied ride.

Total Distance: 4 miles. Your ride can be lengthened via connecting
trails.

Location: Blue Range Wilderness and Primitive Area

Type of Trail: Equestrian/Hiker

Connecting Trails: Grant Cabin Trail #306 (which connects to Grant
Creek Trail #75), Long Cienega Trail #305 at 3.8 miles (which
connects to Steeple Mesa Trail #73), terminus at Paradise Trail #74

Difficulty: Difficult

Elevation: 8,720 to 7,120 feet

Best Months: May through October

Maps: Apache-Sitgreaves National Forest USGS: Hannagan Meadows,
Strayhorse

Special Considerations: No direct road access. The trail is accessed
from the Steeple Trail.

Trailhead: From Alpine, drive south on US 191 23 miles to the south
end of Hannagan Meadows. Turn left (east) to the Steeple Trail
trailhead. Ride 1 mile to the Upper Grant Creek Trail.

McKITTRICK TRAIL #72

Highlights: Beautiful panoramic views.

Total Distance: 5.9 miles. Your ride can be lengthened via connecting
trails.

Location: Blue Ridge Wilderness and Primitive Area

Type of Trail: Equestrian/Hiker

Connecting Trails: Blue Lookout Trail #71 and terminus at 0.8 miles, K-P Trail #70 at 5.9 miles.
Difficulty: Difficult
Elevation: 9,266 to 6,560 feet
Best Months: May through October
Maps: Apache-Sitgreaves National Forest USGS: Strayhorse
Trailhead: From Alpine, travel south on US 191 29 miles to FR 84 (Blue Lookout Road). This is the first left after the road to the Salt House Trail, and is signed "Dead End." Drive east on this primitive road 6.5 miles to an open flat and parking lot. The road is closed after this point.

STEEPLE MESA TRAIL #73

Highlights: The boggy little meadows are called *cienegas*.
Total Distance: 13.2 miles. Your ride can be lengthened via connecting trails.
Location: Blue Ridge Wilderness and Primitive Area
Type of Trail: Equestrian/Hiker
Connecting Trails: Upper Grant Trail #65 in the first of the four *cienegas* at 1.3 miles, Long Cienega Trail #305 at 2.8 miles, K-P Rim Trail #315 at 3.3 miles, Paradise Trail #74 at 6.4 miles, and K-P Trail #70 at 7.7 miles (go through gate on ridge; Steeple Trail goes east along ridgeline).
Difficulty: Difficult
Elevation: 9,200 to 5,280 feet
Best Months: May through October
Maps: Apache-Sitgreaves National Forest USGS: Hannagan Meadows, Strayhorse, Bear Mountain
Special Considerations: Water is usually available at Willow Springs and Mud Springs. Pools in Steeple Creek.
Trailhead: From Alpine, drive south on US 191 23 miles to the south end of Hannagan Meadows and turn left (east) on FR 29A to the Steeple and Foote Creek trailhead and parking lot. Or, from Alpine, take US 180 3 miles east to FR 281 (Blue River Road). Turn south and travel 30 miles to the Blue River Road access to the Steeple Trail.

BLUE CABIN RUINS TRAIL #321

Highlights: On this connecting trail, there is a burned cabin of an alleged bank robber who robbed the McNary Bank in 1921. The man was apprehended at the cabin by the sheriff's posse and shot. The cabin burned in 1980.

Total Distance: 2.9 miles. Your ride can be lengthened via connecting trails.

Location: Blue Ridge Wilderness and Primitive Area

Type of Trail: Equestrian/Hiker

Connecting Trails: Blue Lookout Trail #71, McKittrick Trail #72

Difficulty: Difficult

Elevation: 8,920 to 8,300 feet

Best Months: May through October

Maps: Apache-Sitgreaves National Forest USGS: Strayhorse

Trailhead: From Alpine, drive south on US 191 to FR 84 (Blue Lookout Road). This is the first left after the Salt House Trail and is signed "Dead End." Drive east 6.5 miles on this primitive road; the road ends and there is a dirt parking lot.

TUTT CREEK TRAIL #105

Highlights: Rocky Mountain Bighorn sheep have been seen on the ridges.

Total Distance: 4.2 miles. Your ride can be lengthened via connecting trails.

Location: Blue Ridge Wilderness and Primitive Area

Type of Trail: Equestrian/Hiker

Connecting Trails: Foote Creek Trail #76

Difficulty: Moderate

Elevation: 6,600 to 5,800 feet

Best Months: Year-round

Maps: Apache-Sitgreaves National Forest USGS: Maness

Special Considerations: Cleveland Spring provides water for stock at 3.4 miles.

Trailhead: From Alpine, drive south on US 191 14.5 miles to FR 567 (Red Hill Road). Turn east and follow this road 11 miles as it descends to a jeep trail. Park here and ride 0.5 mile to Blue River.

BLUE LOOKOUT TRAIL #71

Highlights: A connecting trail to Blue Cabin Ruins Trail #321 (1 mile) and K-P Trail #70 (at 2.9 miles). The former features the burned cabin of an alleged bank robber.

Total Distance: 2.9 miles. Your ride can be lengthened via connecting trails.

Location: Blue Range Wilderness and Primitive Area

Type of Trail: Equestrian/Hiker

Connecting Trails: Blue Cabin Ruins Trail #321 at 1 mile, K-P Trail #70 at 2.9 miles

Difficulty: Difficult

Elevation: 9,346 to 6,800 feet

Best Months: May through October

Maps: Apache-Sitgreaves National Forest USGS: Strayhorse

Special Considerations: There is a 5-mile ride from the campground to the junction of K-P and Blue Lookout Trails in K-P Canyon.

Trailhead: From Alpine, drive south on US 191 29 miles to FR 82 (Blue Lookout Road). This road is the first left after the road to the Salt House Trail, and is signed "Dead End." Drive east on this primitive road about 6.5 miles to an open flat area and a dirt parking lot. Follow McKittrick Trail #72 1 mile to its junction with the Blue Lookout Trail.

K-P TRAIL #70

Highlights: A beautiful trail that starts in an alpine meadow, proceeds into a beautiful canyon, and comes back out to high desert. Confluence of the south and north forks of K-P Creek. Waterfalls.

Total Distance: 9.4 miles. Your ride can be lengthened via connecting trails.

Location: Blue Range Wilderness and Primitive Area

Type of Trail: Equestrian/Hiker

Connecting Trails: North Fork Trail #93 at 2.9 miles, Blue Lookout Trail #71 at 5.6 miles, McKittrick Trail #72 at 6.5 miles, terminus at Steeple Mesa Trail #73

Difficulty: Moderate to difficult

Elevation: 8,960 to 6,560 feet

Best Months: May through October

Maps: Apache-Sitgreaves National Forest USGS: Strayhorse, Bear Mountain

Trailhead: From Alpine, drive south on US 191 28 miles to the K-P Cienega Campground Road, then 1.3 miles to the trailhead.

NORTH FORK K-P TRAIL #93

Highlights: A beautiful connecting trail to K-P Trail #70. Cool temperatures. Two 10-foot waterfalls. Confluence of the south and north forks of K-P Creek.

Total Distance: 2.4 miles. Your ride can be lengthened via connecting trails.

Location: Blue Ridge Wilderness and Primitive Area

Type of Trail: Equestrian/Hiker

Connecting Trails: K-P Trail #70

Difficulty: Moderate

Elevation: 9,200 to 7,600 feet

Best Months: May through October

Maps: Apache-Sitgreaves National Forest USGS: Strayhorse

Trailhead: From Alpine, take US 191 south 25 miles to the North Fork K-P/K-P Rim trailhead. This trail is also accessible via K-P Trail #70.

K-P RIM TRAIL #315

Highlights: A short connecting trail to Steeple Mesa Trail #73 with great views of K-P Canyon.

Total Distance: 2.2 miles. Your ride can be lengthened via connecting trails.

Location: Blue Ridge Wilderness and Primitive Area

Type of Trail: Equestrian/Hiker

Connecting Trails: Steeple Mesa Trail #73

Difficulty: Easy

Elevation: 9,280 to 9,100 feet

Best Months: May through October

Maps: Apache-Sitgreaves National Forest USGS: Strayhorse

Special Considerations: At the Steeple Creek Trail junction, a turn
   north and a 3.3-mile ride will bring you to Hannagan Meadows.
Trailhead: From Alpine, take US 191 south 25 miles to the North
   Fork K-P/K-P Rim trailhead.

SOUTH CANYON TRAIL #53

Highlights: This trail follows a circuitous route.
Total Distance: 5.8 miles. Your ride can be lengthened via connecting
   trails.
Location: Blue Range Wilderness and Primitive Area
Type of Trail: Equestrian/Hiker
Connecting Trails: Cow Flat Trail #55, Marks Ranch Trail
Difficulty: Difficult
Elevation: 5,680 to 7,600 feet
Best Months: April through November
Maps: Apache-Sitgreaves National Forest USGS: Blue Mountain
Special Considerations: This trail is also accessible via Cow Flat
   Trail #55.
Trailhead: From Alpine, drive east on US 180 3 miles to FR 281 (Blue
   River Road). Head south and follow this road for 23 miles to the
   Blue Administration Site. The trailhead is denoted as "Lanphier
   Foote Creek, S. Canyon Trail." From the trailhead, proceed to the
   right through two gates to the Blue River. Proceed upstream to the
   north of South Canyon.

LANPHIER TRAIL #52

Highlights: A very scenic route through Blue Range Wilderness and
   Primitive Area.
Total Distance: 5.6 miles. Your ride can be lengthened via connecting
   trails.
Location: Blue Ridge Wilderness and Primitive Area
Type of Trail: Equestrian/Hiker
Connecting Trails: Largo Trail #51, Cow Flat Trail #55
Difficulty: Moderate to difficult
Elevation: 5,600 to 7,360 feet

Best Months: April through November
Maps: Apache-Sitgreaves National Forest USGS: Bear Mountain, Blue Mountain
Special Considerations: The trail follows Lanphier Canyon until it begins to go upslope and joins Cow Flat Trail #55.
Trailhead: From Alpine, drive east on US 180 3 miles to FR 281 (Blue River Road). Turn south and follow this road 23 miles to the Blue Administration Site. The trailhead is marked "Largo and Foote Creek THD." Walk to the right through two gates to the Blue River, about 100 yards downstream. On the opposite side is a corral, which marks the entry to Largo Canyon.

SAWMILL TRAIL #39

Highlights: Most of this trail is located in high desert country.
Total Distance: 5.4 miles. Your ride can be lengthened via connecting trails.
Location: Blue Range Wilderness and Primitive Area
Type of Trail: Equestrian/Hiker
Connecting Trails: WS Lake Trail #54
Difficulty: Moderate to difficult
Elevation: 5,600 to 8,400 feet
Best Months: April through October
Maps: Apache-Sitgreaves National Forest USGS: Bear Mountain
Special Considerations: To reach the summit of Bear Mountain, you will need to continue beyond the junction of the Sawmill and WS Lake Trails. From there, continue on the WS Lake Trail an additional 0.25 mile.
Trailhead: From Alpine, take US 180 east 3.5 miles to FR 281 (Blue River Road). Turn south and follow this road 24.5 miles to the Sawmill trailhead on the left.

FRANZ SPRING TRAIL #43

Highlights: An old livestock trail with an old line cabin built for line riders who checked fence lines of the ranch.

Total Distance: 3 miles. Your ride can be lengthened via connecting trails.
Location: Blue Ridge Wilderness and Primitive Area
Type of Trail: Equestrian/Hiker
Connecting Trails: Bonanza Bill Trail #23
Difficulty: Moderate
Elevation: 7,360 to 8,400 feet
Best Months: April through October
Maps: Apache-Sitgreaves National Forest USGS: Blue SE
Special Considerations: The WS Lake Trail is also called the Whoa Trail by cowboys because of its steep gorge, a good place to say "Whoa." There are no direct access points to the trailhead.
Trailhead: Use the Bonanza Bill trailhead. From Alpine, drive east on US 180 3 miles to FR 281 (Blue River Road). Turn south and follow this scenic back road for 20.7 miles to the Pueblo Park Road (FR 32). The trailhead is 4.7 miles east on this dirt road at the wooden canal.

BONANZA BILL TRAIL #23

Highlights: One of the main trails that provide access to the remote parts of the Blue Range Primitive Area. Excellent view of Devils Monument.
Total Distance: 12.1 miles. Your ride can be lengthened via connecting trails.
Location: Blue Range Wilderness and Primitive Area
Type of Trail: Equestrian/Hiker
Connecting Trails: Tige Rim Trail #90, Hinkle Spring Trail #30, Cow Flat Trail #55, Franz Spring Trail #43
Difficulty: Moderate
Elevation: 7,040 to 8,400 feet
Best Months: April through November
Maps: Apache-Sitgreaves National Forest USGS: Blue
Special Considerations: Trail crosses into New Mexico
Trailhead: From alpine, drive east on US 180 3 miles to FR 281 (Blue River Road). Turn south and follow this scenic back road

20.7 miles to the Pueblo Park Road (FR 232). The trailhead is 4.7 miles east on this dirt road. There is a wooden corral.

LARGO TRAIL #51

Highlights: A major access trail into the eastern Blue Range Wilderness and Primitive Area.

Total Distance: 5.6 miles. Your ride can be lengthened via connecting trails.

Location: Blue Range Wilderness and Primitive Area

Type of Trail: Equestrian/Hiker

Connecting Trails: Lanphier Trail #52, Telephone Ridge Trail, WS Lake Trail #54

Difficulty: Moderate to difficult

Elevation: 5,600 to 7,840 feet

Best Months: April through November

Maps: Apache-Sitgreaves National Forest USGS: Bear Mountain, Blue

Trailhead: From Alpine, drive east on US 180 3 miles to FR 281 (Blue River Road). Turn south and travel 23 miles to the Blue Administration Site and a trailhead marked "Lanphier, Foote Creek, and S. Canyon." From the trailhead, head to the right of the gates to the Blue River; 100 yards farther is the Lanphier Trail. The Largo Trail begins about 0.5 mile up the Lanphier Trail.

BEAR WALLOW TRAIL #63

Highlights: The Bear Wallow area was named by early explorers for the large number of bear wallows found here. Large stand of old-growth ponderosa pine.

Total Distance: 7.6 miles. Your ride can be lengthened via connecting trails.

Location: Bear Wallow Wilderness

Type of Trail: Equestrian/Hiker

Connecting Trails: Gobbler Point Trail #59, Reno Trail #62, Schell Canyon Trail #316, Rose Spring Trail #309

Difficulty: Moderate to difficult

Elevation: 8,700 to 6,700 feet

Best Months: May through October
Maps: Apache-Sitgreaves National Forest USGS: Baldy Bill, Hoodoo
  Knoll
Special Considerations: You will need a permit to travel on the San
  Carlos Apache Indian Reservation. See page 4 for the address.
  Watch out for poison ivy.
Trailhead: From Alpine, drive south on US 191 about 28 miles to
  FR 25. Turn west and travel 2.8 miles to the Bear Wallow trailhead.
  This trail is also accessible from Gobbler Point Trail #59, Reno
  Trail #62, Schell Canyon Trail #316, and Rose Spring Trail #309.

GOBBLER POINT TRAIL #59

Highlights: A connecting trail with old-growth forests.
Total Distance: 2.7 miles. Your ride can be lengthened via connecting
  trails.
Location: Bear Wallow Wilderness
Type of Trail: Equestrian/Hiker
Connecting Trails: Bear Wallow Trail #63
Difficulty: Difficult
Elevation: 8,770 to 6,700 feet
Best Months: Spring through fall
Maps: Apache-Sitgreaves National Forest USGS: Hoodoo Knoll
Special Considerations: This steep trail drops 2,100 feet in 2.7 miles.
Trailhead: From Alpine, drive south on US 191 28 miles to FR 25.
  Head west on FR 25 to Gobbler Point Road 8154 on the left (south)
  side of FR 25. Take this road left at the first fork and right at the
  second fork. Drive 3 miles to the trailhead.

THREE FORKS TO DIAMOND ROCK TRAIL #81

Highlights: Multiple river crossings. This is a fisherman's path rather
  than a developed trail, but is still a lovely ride.
Total Distance: 4.7 miles
Location: Outer White Mountains
Type of Trail: Equestrian/Hiker
Difficulty: Easy

Elevation: 8,200 to 7,900 feet
Best Months: May through October
Maps: Apache-Sitgreaves National Forest USGS: Buffalo Crossing
Trailhead: From Alpine, drive north on US 191 1.5 miles to FR 249.
Turn west and follow FR 249 10.6 miles to Three Forks. For access
to the downstream portion of this trail, take US 666 about 5 miles
to FR 249. Follow FR 249 to FR 276. Turn south and continue
6 miles to the Diamond Rock Campground. Head upstream to
Three Forks.

FISH CREEK ACCESS TRAIL #320 AND FISH CREEK TRAIL #60

Highlights: This creek path was restored in part by the Arizona
Chapter of the Sierra Club. Fish Creek is home to the Apache
trout. It is a pleasant ride. At 5.5 miles is the confluence with Fish
Creek and Black River. Trout fishing.
Total Distance: 5.5 miles
Location: Outer White Mountains
Type of Trail: Equestrian/Hiker
Difficulty: Moderate
Elevation: 8,400 to 6,800 feet
Best Months: May through October
Maps: Apache-Sitgreaves National Forest USGS: Hoodoo Knoll
Trailhead: From Alpine, drive south on US 191 14.5 miles to FR 26.
Turn right and follow FR 26 about 9.5 miles to FR 24. Turn right
and follow FR 24 to FR 83. Turn right and follow FR 83 for 3 miles
to FR 83A, which turns right in about 1.4 miles to a lesser dirt road
that forks left. Follow this road about 0.5 mile past the old corral
to the #320 trailhead, or proceed 0.6 mile farther to Fish Creek
Trail #60.

ESCUDILLA NATIONAL RECREATION TRAIL #308

Highlights: An easy trail with magnificent views and a good oppor-
tunity to view a forest ecosystem in transition. The wildfire of 1951
killed much of the vegetation. The extensive natural reclaiming has

led to this area's designation as a National Research Area. There is a fire tower on the summit of Mt. Escudilla. Magnificent fall colors with the aspen.

Total Distance: 3 miles. Your ride can be lengthened via connecting trails.

Location: Escudilla Wilderness

Type of Trail: Equestrian/Hiker

Connecting Trails: Government Trail #119

Difficulty: Easy

Elevation: 9,560 to 10,877 feet

Best Months: May through October

Maps: Apache-Sitgreaves National Forest USGS: Escudilla

Special Considerations: Summer thundershowers may be severe.

Trailhead: From Alpine, drive north on US 191 5.5 to 6 miles to FR 56. Turn right on FR 56 and proceed 3.6 miles to Terry Flat. Take the left fork past Tool Box Draw to the trailhead.

MAINSTEM BLACK RIVER TRAIL

Highlights: A beautiful but popular trail with good trout fishing. Reputed to be one of the most scenic streams in the Southwest. At 11 miles is the Centerfire Creek confluence. At 12.9 miles is Wildcat Bridge.

Total Distance: 19 miles. Your ride can be lengthened via connecting trails.

Location: Escudilla Wilderness

Type of Trail: Equestrian/Hiker

Connecting Trails: Fish Creek Access Trail #320, Fish Creek Trail #60, Bear Creek Trail

Difficulty: Easy

Elevation: 7,500 to 6,600 feet

Best Months: May through October

Maps: Apache-Sitgreaves National Forest USGS: Buffalo Crossing, Hannagan, Hoodoo Knoll

Special Conditions: At 19 miles, the trail ends at the San Carlos Apache Reservation. Please respect their boundaries and law.

Trailhead: From Alpine, travel south on US 191 14.5 miles to FR 26. Turn right and follow FR 26 about 9.5 miles to FR 24. At this point, you can turn left (southwest) and go 1.5 miles to Bear Creek; or turn right (northeast) and go 3 miles to FR 25 and then left, continuing 1.5 miles to Buffalo Crossing with access to unmaintained trail. FR 25 continues 12.8 miles to Wildcat Bridge.

GOVERNMENT TRAIL #119

Highlights: This connecting trail is an excellent trail to discover Escudilla Mountain, Arizona's third tallest mountain. This trail joins the Escudilla National Recreation Trail on Profanity Ridge. This is a historic trail used by Forest Service workers to get to the Forest Service tower.

Total Distance: 2.9 miles

Location: Escudilla Wilderness

Type of Trail: Equestrian/Hiker; Mountain bikers up to the wilderness area only

Connecting Trails: Escudilla National Recreation Trail #308 at 2.9 miles

Difficulty: Difficult

Elevation: 9,200 to 10,877 feet

Best Months: May through October

Maps: Apache-Sitgreaves National Forest USGS: Nutrioso

Special Considerations: Extensive Aspen forests show their golden color the first week of October. There are steep talus-covered switchbacks.

Trailhead: From Alpine, travel north on US 191 5.5 to 6 miles to FR 56. Turn east on this dirt road and travel 1.6 miles. The road is closed past this point.

Chevelon Ranger District

GENERAL GEORGE CROOK TRAIL
(HIGHLINE TRAIL #47)

Highlights: A historic trail named after and built under the command
of General George Crook. This trail, originally 200 but now 138
miles long, passes along the Mogollon Rim and through the jurisdiction of three national forests. The trail was originally built to provide a supply route from Ft. Whipple (near Prescott) to Ft. Apache
(in White River).

Total Distance: 13.5 miles

Location: Mogollon Rim

Type of Trail: Equestrian/Hiker

Connecting Trails: Drew Trail #291, Myrtle Trail #30, Horton Spring
Trail #292, Clark Trail #143, Geronimo Trail #240, Turkey Springs
Trail #217, Webster Trail #228, East Weber Trail #289, Pine Canyon
Trail #226, Railroad Tunnel Trail #390

Difficulty: Moderate

Elevation: 7,500 to 7,900 feet

Best Months: Year-round

Maps: Apache-Sitgreaves National Forest USGS: Woods Canyon,
Heber, Clay Springs

Special Considerations: The trail merges with FR 300 on the rim.
There is no potable water. There may be snow in winter at the
higher elevations.

Trailhead: Off AZ 260 between Payson and Show Low

Clifton Ranger District

WAR FINANCE TRAIL #9

Highlights: A moderately sloped and forested trail connecting to
Robinson Mesa.

Total Distance: 2.7 miles. Your ride can be lengthened via connecting
trails.

Location: White Mountains

Type of Trail: Equestrian/Hiker/Mountain Biker

Connecting Trails: Robinson Mesa Trail #27, Hot Air Trail #18,
Strayhorse Trail #32, Sawmill Cabin Trail, East Eagle Trail #33

Difficulty: Difficult

Elevation: 6,100 to 7,200 feet

Best Months: Spring through fall

Maps: Apache-Sitgreaves National Forest USGS: Robinson Mesa,
Hannagan

Trailhead: Access to this trail is via the Honeymoon Campground,
Robinson Mesa Trail #27, and East Eagle Trail #33. To access the
East Eagle Trail, travel north from Clifton on US 191 for 67 miles
to the trail sign. Turn left onto the dirt road, and proceed 0.3 mile
to the trailhead. To access the Honeymoon Campground, travel
northwest from Clifton on US 191 for 50 miles to FR 217. Turn
left and follow FR 217 to the Honeymoon Campground.

HIGHLINE TRAIL #47

Highlights: A pleasant trail with multiple possibilities for varied
rides. Saunders Cabin on a connecting trail.

Total Distance: 14.6 miles. Your ride can be lengthened via connecting trails.

Location: White Mountains

Type of Trail: Equestrian/Hiker

Connecting Trails: Trail #348, Crabtree Trail #22, Salt House Trail #18,
Chitty Trail #37, McBride Mesa Trail #26, Helispot Trail #166
and #167, Squirrel Trail #34, Dry Prong Trail #45, Warren Canyon
Trail #48, Rim Trail #309

Difficulty: Difficult

Elevation: 7,000 to 7,600 feet

Best Months: Spring through fall

Maps: Apache-Sitgreaves National Forest USGS: Hannagan

Special Considerations: Raspberry Trail #35 begins on the opposite side of the road from the trailhead.

Trailhead: From Clifton, drive north on US 191 for 61 miles to the Stray Horse Campground. The trail starts on the west side of the highway, at the north end of the campground.

SALTHOUSE TRAIL #18

Highlights: A trail connecting East Eagle Trail #33 with the main highway. Elk are usually in this area.

Total Distance: 6.6 miles. Your ride can be lengthened via connecting trails.

Location: White Mountains

Type of Trail: Equestrian/Hiker

Connecting Trails: Highline Trail #47, East Eagle Trail #33, Chitty Creek Trail #37

Difficulty: Difficult

Elevation: 6,000 to 9,200 feet

Best Months: Spring through fall

Maps: Apache-Sitgreaves National Forest USGS: Strayhorse

Special Considerations: This trail is quite steep at the upper end and gentle along East Eagle Creek.

Trailhead: From Clifton, travel north on US 191 to the trail sign just to the northwest of Blue Vista.

SHEEP SADDLE TRAIL #16

Highlights: A short connecting trail generally used by hunters. It connects Hot Air Trail #15 and Hot Air Spur Trail #91 to the main highway.

Total Distance: 1.4 miles. Your ride can be lengthened via connecting trails.

Location: White Mountains

Type of Trail: Equestrian/Hiker
Connecting Trails: Hot Air Trail #15, Hot Air Spur Trail #91
Difficulty: Moderate
Elevation: 7,500 to 6,500 feet
Best Months: Spring through fall
Maps: Apache-Sitgreaves National Forest USGS: Robinson Mesa
Special Considerations: Water is not available.
Trailhead: From Clifton, drive north on US 191 for 53 miles. The
    trail is on the left (west) side of the road.

ROBINSON MESA TRAIL #27

Highlights: A pleasant and easy trail from Eagle Creek to Robinson
    Mesa. Multiple connecting trails.
Total Distance: 10.9 miles. Your ride can be lengthened via connect-
    ing trails.
Location: White Mountains
Type of Trail: Equestrian/Hiker
Connecting Trails: War Finance Trail #9, Hot Air Spur Trail #91,
    Mud Spring Trail #49, Bear Spring Trail #19, Hot Air Trail #15
Difficulty: Easy
Elevation: 7,000 to 8,200 feet
Best Months: Spring through fall
Maps: Apache-Sitgreaves National Forest USGS: Robinson Mesa,
    Rose Peak
Trailhead: From Clifton, travel north on US 191 to Rose Peak. The
    trail begins just north of Rose Peak.

SPUR CROSS TRAIL #8

Highlights: This trail accesses the old Spur Cross Homestead, which
    is on private land. Please respect the landowner's privacy. A pre-
    historic cave about 4 miles down the trail.
Total Distance: 5.8 miles. Your ride can be lengthened via connecting
    trails.
Location: White Mountains

Type of Trail: Equestrian/Hiker
Connecting Trails: Painted Bluff Trail #13
Difficulty: Difficult
Elevation: 4,800 to 6,900 feet
Best Months: Year-round
Maps: Apache-Sitgreaves National Forest USGS: Clifton
Trailhead: From Clifton, travel north on US 191 for 21 miles. The trail starts on the west side of the highway about 1 mile north of the Granville Campground.

CHITTY TRAIL #37

Highlights: Great fall colors, plus a waterfall at the junction with Highline Trail #47. This trail ends in Chitty Creek Canyon at a large bubbling spring. Most riders take Trail #37 to the end, then Highline Trail #47 to McBride Mesa Trail #26, and travel over the top on that trail.
Total Distance: 5.2 miles. Your ride can be lengthened via connecting trails.
Location: White Mountains
Type of Trail: Equestrian/Hiker
Connecting Trails: Salthouse Trail #18, McBride Mesa Trail #26, Highline Trail #47
Difficulty: Difficult
Elevation: 6,000 to 7,600 feet
Best Months: Spring through fall
Maps: Apache-Sitgreaves National Forest USGS: Hannagan
Special Considerations: No trailhead, but good backcountry trail access. If coming from the southern access, you will find the remains of Sawmill Cabin.
Trailhead: You can access this trail only from other backcountry trails. The southern access is via Salthouse Trail #18. The northern access is via Highline Trail #47. See page 27 for access to Highline Trail #47 or page 27 for access to Salthouse Trail #18 and East Eagle Trail #33. Refer to page 33 for East Eagle Trail trailhead access.

RED MOUNTAIN TRAIL #25

Highlights: Good fall color in October. In summer it is common to find millions of swarming ladybugs at higher elevations.

Total Distance: 6.8 miles. Your ride can be lengthened via connecting trails.

Location: White Mountains

Type of Trail: Equestrian/Hiker

Connecting Trails: Strayhorse Trail #32

Difficulty: Difficult

Elevation: 6,800 to 8,000 feet

Best Months: Spring through fall

Maps: Apache-Sitgreaves National Forest USGS: Rose Peak

Trailhead: From Clifton, drive north on US 191 to the Rose Peak turnoff. Follow the old road around to the north side. The trail begins in about 1 mile.

BEAR VALLEY TRAIL #55

Highlights: An old shack and several small waterfalls. The trail travels through a burn area (1993), giving you a chance to see nature healing itself.

Total Distance: 12.1 miles. Your ride can be lengthened via connecting trails.

Location: Blue Range Primitive Area

Type of Trail: Equestrian/Hiker/Mountain Biker

Connecting Trails: Bonanza Bill #23, South Canyon Trail #53, Franz Spring Trail #43, Lanphier Trail #52, WS Lake Trail #54, Little Blue Trail #41

Difficulty: Moderate

Elevation: 7,600 to 4,800 feet

Best Months: Spring through fall

Maps: Apache-Sitgreaves National Forest USGS: Alma Mesa, Blue

Special Considerations: The trail is hard to follow from Bear Valley to the Blue River. Bring a map and compass. Follow rock cairns and blazes, not the drainage, out of Auger Tank.

Trailhead: You will need to use the Bonanza Bill trailhead at Bonanza Flat. From Alpine, drive 3 miles east on US 180 to FR 281 (Blue

River Road). Turn south and follow this scenic back road 20.7 miles to the Pueblo Park Road (FR 232). The trailhead is 4.7 miles east on this dirt road; there is a wooden corral.

McBride Mesa Trail #26

Highlights: A grassy ride. The lower two-thirds of the trail is through juniper and piñon. Backcountry access from Dry Prong Trail #45.

Total Distance: 9.4 miles. Your ride can be lengthened via connecting trails.

Location: White Mountains

Type of Trail: Equestrian/Hiker

Connecting Trails: Highline Trail #47, M-C Trail #462, East Eagle Trail #33, Squirrel Canyon Trail #34, Raspberry Trail #35, Dry Prong Trail #45

Difficulty: Moderate

Elevation: 9,000 to 6,200 feet

Best Months: Spring through fall

Maps: Apache-Sitgreaves National Forest USGS: Hannagan, Robinson Mesa

Trailhead: You will need to use the trailhead on FR 54D. This trailhead is shared by other trails. To access FR 54 from Clifton, take US 191 north for 68 miles to FR 54. Take FR 54 west for 5 miles to the signed junction with FR 54D. Drive 0.25 mile farther to the trailhead. Ride down FR 54D 1 mile, where this trail leaves the road. To access FR 54D from Alpine, take US 191 south for 29 miles to FR 54. Take FR 54 west for 5 miles to the signed junction with FR 54D. Drive 0.25 mile to the trailhead. From the trailhead, ride down FR 54D until the trail leaves the road at 1 mile.

Squirrel Trail #34

Highlights: This trail was relocated and reconstructed to provide access for horse trailers. Beautiful views of aspen. Multiple connecting trails, and a generally reliable spring. Saunders Cabin.

Total Distance: 8.8 miles. Your ride can be lengthened via connecting trails.

Location: White Mountains
Type of Trail: Equestrian/Hiker
Connecting Trails: Highline Trail #47, Warren Canyon Trail #48, East Eagle Trail #33, McBride Mesa Trail #26
Difficulty: Difficult
Elevation: 5,800 to 8,000 feet
Best Months: Spring through fall
Maps: Apache-Sitgreaves National Forest USGS: Hannagan
Special Considerations: Horses and pack animals are not recommended on the upper or last mile.
Trailhead: You will need to use the trailhead on FR 54D. This trailhead is shared by other trails. To access FR 54 from Clifton, take US 191 north for 68 miles to FR 54. Take FR 54 west for 5 miles to the signed junction with FR 54D. Drive 0.25 mile farther to the trailhead. Ride down FR 54D 1 mile, where this trail leaves the road. To access FR 54D from Alpine, take US 191 south for 29 miles to FR 54. Take FR 54 W for 5 miles to the signed junction with FR 54D. Drive 0.25 mile to the trailhead. From the trailhead, ride down FR 54D until the trail leaves the road at 1 mile.

HOT AIR TRAIL #18

Highlights: This trail follows the Canyon Bottom Trail and the Hot Air Creek Trail, and then climbs to the Rose Peak Trail.
Total Distance: 5.2 miles. Your ride can be lengthened via connecting trails.
Location: White Mountains
Type of Trail: Equestrian/Hiker
Connecting Trails: East Eagle Trail #33, Hot Air Spur Trail #91, Sheep Saddle Trail #16, Robinson Mesa Trail #27
Difficulty: Difficult
Elevation: 8,400 to 6,200 feet
Best Months: Spring through December
Maps: Apache-Sitgreaves National Forest USGS: Robinson Mesa. Rose Peak

Special Considerations: The Canyon Bottom Trail can be rough and difficult to follow at times because of the ever-changing streambed.

Trailhead: From Clifton, travel north on US 191 to Rose Peak. The trailhead is at the Rose Peak turnoff.

EAST EAGLE TRAIL #33

Highlights: A pleasant, gentle trail that passes the Sawmill Cabin. Multiple connecting trails.

Total Distance: 12.6 miles. Your ride can be lengthened via connecting trails.

Location: White Mountains

Type of Trail: Equestrian/Hiker

Connecting Trails: Salthouse Trail #18, Hot Air Trail #15, Crabtree Trail #22, Dry Prong Trail #45, McBride Mesa Trail #26

Difficulty: Easy to moderate

Elevation: 6,000 to 7,200 feet

Best Months: Spring through December

Maps: Apache-Sitgreaves National Forest USGS: Hannagan

Trailhead: From Clifton, travel north on US 191 for 67 miles to the trail sign. Turn left onto the dirt road, and proceed 0.3 mile to the trailhead.

HOT AIR SPUR TRAIL #91

Highlights: This connecting trail traverses the west fork of Hot Air Canyon. The slopes and ridges of this area are part of the winter range for local elk.

Total Distance: 1.2 miles. Your ride can be lengthened via connecting trails.

Location: White Mountains

Type of Trail: Equestrian/Hiker

Connecting Trails: Robinson Mesa Trail #27, Hot Air Trail #18, Sheep Saddle Trail #16

Difficulty: Difficult

Elevation: 6,800 to 6,400 feet

Best Months: Spring through December
Maps: Apache-Sitgreaves National Forest USGS: Robinson Mesa
Trailhead: This trail is accessible from two points in the backcountry: Hot Air Trail #18 and Sheep Saddle Trail #16. To get to Sheep Saddle Trail #16 from Clifton, drive north on US 191 for 53 miles. The trail is on the left (west) side of the road.

H.L. Canyon Trail #11

Highlights: An excellent short loop trail with both trailheads on US 191.
Total Distance: 5 miles. Your ride can be lengthened via connecting trails.
Location: White Mountains
Type of Trail: Equestrian/Hiker
Connecting Trails: Sardine Saddle Trail #572, Big Tree Trail #300, Frye Trail #12, Connect Trail #703, Trail #312
Difficulty: Difficult
Elevation: 7,200 to 7,300 feet
Best Months: Spring through fall
Maps: Apache-Sitgreaves National Forest USGS: Clifton
Trailhead: From Clifton, travel north on US 191 for 23 miles. You will see the trailhead sign on the east side of the road. Sardine Saddle Trail #572 and Big Tree Trail #300 start across the road.

Strayhorse Canyon Trail #20

Highlights: This trail connects with and provides access to a multitude of other trails. Old cabins.
Total Distance: 9.4 miles. Your ride can be lengthened via connecting trails.
Location: Blue Range Primitive Area
Type of Trail: Equestrian/Hiker
Connecting Trails: Hagan Trail #31, Lengthy Trail #89, Red Mountain Trail #25, Blue River Trail #101

Difficulty: Moderate
Elevation: 8,200 to 8,300 feet
Best Months: Spring through December
Maps: Apache-Sitgreaves National Forest USGS: Rose Peak, Dutch Blue
Special Considerations: Water is usually not available. There may be water in Strayhorse Spring.
Trailhead: From Clifton, drive north on US 191 for 49 miles. The trailhead is on the east side of the road. The trailhead is shared with Red Mountain Trail #25.

WARREN CANYON TRAIL #48

Highlights: Connects Highline Trail #47 at Saunders Cabin with Dry Prong Trail #45.
Total Distance: 3.2 miles. Your ride can be lengthened via connecting trails.
Location: White Mountains
Type of Trail: Equestrian/Hiker
Connecting Trails: Highline Trail #47, Dry Prong Trail #45
Difficulty: Difficult
Elevation: 5,800 to 6,600 feet
Best Months: Spring through December
Maps: Apache-Sitgreaves National Forest USGS: Baldy Bill Point
Trailhead: This connecting trail is accessed backcountry via Highline Trail #47. From Clifton, drive north on US 191 for 61 miles to the Stray Horse Campground. The trail starts on the west side of the highway, at the north end of the campground.

WILDBUNCH TRAIL #7

Highlights: Reconstructed in 1997, this access trail to the Blue River via Horse Canyon Trail #36 is quite remote.
Total Distance: 11.3 miles. Your ride can be lengthened via connecting trails.

Location: White Mountains
Type of Trail: Equestrian/Hiker
Connecting Trails: Horse Canyon Trail #36
Difficulty: Difficult
Elevation: 4,800 to 7,200 feet
Best Months: April through December
Maps: Apache-Sitgreaves National Forest USGS: Fritz Canyon,
  Maple Peak
Special Considerations: Do not attempt to reach this trail without a
  four-wheel-drive. The road is very rough. If it is too rough, ride
  FR 475 instead.
Trailhead: From Alpine, travel south on the Juan Miller Road
  (FR 475) approximately 1 mile from the Blue River. FR 475
  becomes FR 475C, and then begins to drop into Blue River
  Canyon. After crossing the river, the trail branches off the road
  (475 C) and heads north.

AD BAR TRAIL #14

Highlights: This trail passes the VT Cabin at about 8 miles and then
  continues east to HU Bar Cabin on the Blue River. Both cabins are
  of historical value.
Total Distance: 12 miles
Location: Blue Ridge Wilderness and Primitive Area
Type of Trail: Equestrian/Hiker
Connecting Trails: Burns Trail #547
Difficulty: Difficult
Elevation: 7,000 to 5,600 feet
Best Months: May through November
Maps: Apache-Sitgreaves National Forest USGS: Rose Peak 325NE,
  Dutch Blue Creek 326NW
Special Considerations: May be very hazardous in the winter.
  Limited trailhead parking for horse trailers.
Trailhead: From Clifton, take US 191 north for 42 miles. Parking is
  on the west side. The trail begins on the left side.

BEAR SPRING TRAIL #19

Highlights: This trail provides access to Eagle Creek and/or access to the top of the Mogollon Rim through connections to other trails. It also provides access to the East Eagle Recreational Trail.

Total Distance: 4.4 miles. Your ride can be lengthened via connecting trails.

Location: White Mountains

Type of Trail: Equestrian/Hiker

Connecting Trails: Bear Canyon Trail #46, Robinson Mesa Trail #27

Difficulty: Difficult

Elevation: 7,900 to 7,000 feet

Best Months: April through December

Maps: Apache-Sitgreaves National Forest USGS: Robinson Mesa

Trailhead: From Clifton, take US 191 north to Rose Peak. The trail begins near Rose Peak.

Heber Ranger District

GENERAL GEORGE CROOK TRAIL (HIGHLINE TRAIL #47)

Highlights: This lightly used trail is marked with white chevrons attached to trees where the trail follows the old roadbed and portions of FR 300. See page 25 for more information.

Total Distance: 44 miles

Location: Military Sink Hole

Type of Trail: Equestrian/Hiker

Connecting Trails: Drew Trail #291, Myrtle Trail #30, Horton Spring Trail #292, Clark Trail #143, Geronimo Trail #240, Turkey Springs Trail #217, Webster Trail #228, East Weber Trail #289, Pine Canyon Trail #226, Railroad Tunnel Trail #390

Difficulty: Moderate

Elevation: 7,800 to 6,500 feet

Best Months: Year-round

Maps: Apache-Sitgreaves National Forest USGS: Woods Canyon, Heber, Clay Springs

Special Considerations: No potable water. Summer thunderstorms can be severe.

Trailhead: At Military Sink Hole. FR 300 ends west of Clay Springs on AZ 260 near milepost 113

Lakeside Ranger District

COUNTRY CLUB TRAIL #632

Highlights: This trail loops through ponderosa pine forests and Whitcomb Spring Meadow. There is a spur to the top of Pat Mullen Mountain.

Total Distance: 3.5 miles. Your ride can be lengthened via connecting trails.

Location: White Mountains

Type of Trail: Equestrian/Hiker/Mountain Biker

Connecting Trails: Country Club/Los Burros Connector Trail #631 at 6.5 miles, Trail #632A to connect to the Springs Trail at 1.3 miles

Difficulty: Moderate

Elevation: 7,190 to 7,612 feet

Best Months: Year-round

Maps: Apache-Sitgreaves National Forest USGS: Lakeside 256NW, Sponseller 256NE, McNary 256SE

Trailhead: From the Lakeside Ranger Station, travel south on AZ 260. Turn left at Bucksprings Road, and left again on FR 182. The trailhead is 2 miles ahead at the junction of FR 185.

FOUR SPRINGS TRAIL #629A

Highlights: A lookout tower on the summit of Lake Mountain. A historic sheep-dipping vat at Dipping Vat Springs.

Total Distance: 8 miles. Your ride can be lengthened via connecting trails.

Location: White Mountains

Type of Trail: Equestrian/Hiker/Mountain Biker

Connecting Trails: Los Burros Trail #631, Land of the Pioneers Trail #629

Difficulty: Moderate

Elevation: 8,500 to 7,500 feet

Best Months: Year-round

Maps: Apache-Sitgreaves National Forest USGS: Sponseller 256NE

Special Considerations: Some snow may be encountered. There is no
   direct access to this trail; backcountry access only. Trail access from
   the Land of the Pioneers trailhead or the Los Burros trailhead.

Trailhead: To access from Land of Pioneers, from Show Low, drive
   east on AZ 60 for 19.5 miles. Turn south on FR 224 (through
   Vernon). Go west on FR 5. The trailhead is 0.5 mile ahead of
   Mount L. To access from Los Burros, from Lakeside, travel south
   on AZ 260 to the town of McNary. Turn north on FR 224 and go
   7.1 miles. Turn right at Los Burros Campground; the trailhead is at
   the far end of the campground.

ICE CAVE TRAIL/BLUE RIDGE CAVE TRAIL #608

Highlights: This trail winds its way along Porter Creek and Scott
   Reservoir before connecting to Blue Ridge Trail #107. Midway
   along the trail is the cave, which is actually a lava tube with a con-
   stant flow of 52-degree air.

Total Distance: 3.5 miles. Your ride can be lengthened via connecting
   trails.

Location: White Mountains

Type of Trail: Equestrian/Hiker/Mountain Biker

Connecting Trails: Blue Ridge Trail #107

Difficulty: Moderate

Elevation: 6,700 to 7,200 feet

Best Months: Year-round

Maps: Apache-Sitgreaves National Forest USGS: Lakeside 256NW

Trailhead: From the Lakeside Ranger Station, travel south on AZ 260.
   Turn left on Porter Mountain Road (FR 45) and go 1 mile. The
   trailhead is on the right.

GHOST OF THE COYOTE TRAIL #641

Highlights: This trail winds through juniper and pine forests. Many
   tanks along the trail provide opportunities to see wildlife.

Total Distance: 16 miles

Location: White Mountains
Type of Trail: Equestrian/Hiker/Mountain Biker
Difficulty: Moderate
Elevation: 6,200 to 6,600 feet
Best Months: Year-round
Maps: Apache-Sitgreaves National Forest USGS: Pinedale 234SW
Special Considerations: This can be a long hot day ride in the summer.
Trailhead: From the Show Low Post Office, travel west on AZ 260
    for 8.1 miles to Burten Road. Turn north and the trailhead is
    1.1 miles farther on the left side of the road.

BLUE RIDGE TRAIL #107

Highlights: This loop trail follows Billy Creek and winds through
    ponderosa pine forests.
Total Distance: 8.7 miles. Your ride can be lengthened via connecting
    trails.
Location: White Mountains
Type of Trail: Equestrian/Hiker/Mountain Biker
Connecting Trails: Spring Trail #633, Ice Cave Trail #608
Difficulty: Moderate
Elevation: 6,700 to 7,200 feet
Best Months: Year-round
Maps: Apache-Sitgreaves National Forest USGS: Lakeside 256NW
Trailhead: From Lakeside, travel east on Buck Springs Road (AZ 260).
    Turn north on FR 182 and then west on FR 187 to trailhead #2.
    Trailhead #1 is farther down the road.

PANORAMA TRAIL #635

Highlights: This loop trail passes through the Woolhouse Wildlife
    Habitat Area. Great views.
Total Distance: 8 miles. Your ride can be lengthened via connecting
    trails.
Location: White Mountains

Type of Trail: Equestrian/Hiker/Mountain Biker
Connecting Trails: Trails #636A and #636B, which connect to Timber Mesa Trail #636
Difficulty: Moderate
Elevation: 6,750 to 7,300 feet
Best Months: Year-round
Maps: Apache-Sitgreaves National Forest USGS: Lakeside 256NW
Trailhead: From the Lakeside Ranger Station travel south on AZ 260. Turn left on Porter Mountain Road (FR 45), and travel 6 miles to the trailhead on the left.

BUENA VISTA TRAIL #637

Highlights: This loop trail follows portions of an old logging trail and offers impressive views. The terrain is relatively hilly, but not a problem for horses.
Total Distance: 9 miles
Location: White Mountains
Type of Trail: Equestrian/Hiker/Mountain Biker
Difficulty: Moderate
Elevation: 6,520 to 6,773 feet
Best Months: Year-round
Maps: Apache-Sitgreaves National Forest USGS: Show Low South 255NE
Trailhead: From the Show Low Post Office, travel south on AZ 60 about 4.5 miles. Turn left on FR 300. The trailhead is on the left.

LOS CABALLOS TRAIL #638

Highlights: This loop trail is on relatively easy flat ground with the exception of a few short steep climbs.
Total Distance: 14 miles
Location: White Mountains
Type of Trail: Equestrian/Hiker/Mountain Biker
Difficulty: Moderate to difficult

Elevation: 6,300 to 6,940 feet

Best Months: Year-round

Maps: Apache-Sitgreaves National Forest USGS: Red Top Mountain 255NW, Show Low North 234SE, Show Low South 255NE, Pinedale 234SE

Trailhead: From the Show Low Post Office, travel west on AZ 260 for 3.9 miles. Turn left on FR 136. The trailhead is 0.6 mile ahead on the right.

JUNIPER RIDGE TRAIL #640

Highlights: The lookout tower is open during the summer.

Total Distance: 14 miles (loop), 7.2 miles (shortcut loop).

Location: White Mountains

Type of Trail: Equestrian/Hiker/Mountain Biker

Connecting Trails: General George Crook Trail

Difficulty: Difficult

Elevation: 6,370 to 6,998 feet

Best Months: Year-round

Maps: Apache-Sitgreaves National Forest USGS: Pinedale 234SW

Trailhead: From the Show Low Post Office, travel west on AZ 260 for 11 miles and turn right on Old Highway 260. Turn left on 160 and go 2 miles. The trailhead is on the right.

LOS BURROS TRAIL #631

Highlights: This loop trail passes through beautiful aspen groves and ponderosa pines. The Los Burros Campground is the former site of the Los Burros Ranger Station.

Total Distance: 13 miles. Your ride can be lengthened via connecting trails.

Location: White Mountains

Type of Trail: Equestrian/Hiker/Mountain Biker

Connecting Trails: Trail #631B and Trail #631A connect to Country Club Trail #632.

Difficulty: Moderate

Elevation: 7,800 to 8,370 feet

Best Months: Year-round

Maps: Apache-Sitgreaves National Forest USGS: Sponseller 256NE, McNary 256NE, Boundary Butte 257NW

Trailhead: From Lakeside, travel south on AZ 260 to McNary. Go north on FR 224 for 7.1 miles. Turn into Los Burros Campground; the trailhead is at the far end of the campground.

LAND OF THE PIONEERS TRAIL #629

Highlights: This loop trail travels through ponderosa pine forests to the summit of Ecks Mountain.

Total Distance: 11 miles. Your ride can be lengthened via connecting trails.

Location: White Mountains

Type of Trail: Equestrian/Hiker/Mountain Biker

Connecting Trails: Los Burros Trail #631 via Four Springs Trail #629A

Difficulty: Difficult

Elevation: 7,220 to 7,866 feet

Best Months: Year-round

Maps: Apache-Sitgreaves National Forest USGS: Sponseller 256NE, Boundary Butte 257NW

Special Considerations: Parking is limited at the trailhead.

Trailhead: From Show Low, travel east on AZ 260 for 19.4 miles. Turn south on FR 224 (through Vernon) and go 5 miles. Turn west on FR 5. The trailhead is on the right 0.5 mile ahead.

TIMBER MESA TRAIL #636

Highlights: This loop trail follows the top edge of the mesa, looping back along Chimneys' Fire Road.

Total Distance: 6 miles. Your ride can be lengthened via connecting trails.

Location: White Mountains

Type of Trail: Equestrian/Hiker/Mountain Biker

Connecting Trails: Sawmill Trail #636A or Flume Connector #636B
connects to Panorama Trail #635.

Difficulty: Moderate

Elevation: 6,640 to 6,960 feet

Best Months: Year-round

Maps: Apache-Sitgreaves National Forest USGS: Lakeside 256NW

Special Considerations: Connectors to Sawmill Trail #636A and
Flume #636B, which cross the top of Timber Mesa, one to the
north of Porter Mountain and one to the south. The Sawmill
Connector, at 4 miles, passes the old sawmill at Frost Canyon.
The Flume Connector, at 2.5 miles, is named for the old flume
(pipe), which carried irrigation water.

Trailhead: From the Lakeside Ranger Station, travel south on AZ 260.
Turn left on Porter Mountain Road (FR 45) and go 2.2 miles. Turn
left at the cattle guard and continue to the trailhead on the right.

Springerville Ranger District

RAILROAD GRADE TRAIL #601

Highlights: This trail follows a historic railroad route. Logs were hauled by the railroad in the early years. Later, passengers (tourists) were taken from McNary on tours of the White Mountains. A trestle bridge about 80 feet long is similar to those used by the railroads at the turn of the twentieth century. The ride is easy, with graduated grades and scenic beauty.

Total Distance: 21 miles. Your ride can be lengthened via connecting trails.

Location: Big Lake Area

Type of Trail: Equestrian/Hiker/Mountain Biker

Connecting Trails: Railroad Cave Trail, Lightning Ridge Trail, Sheeps Crossing Trail, Big Cienega

Difficulty: Easy

Elevation: 9,100 to 9,000 feet

Best Months: May through October

Maps: Apache-Sitgreaves National Forest USGS: Big Lake North–280NW Big Lake, AZ

Trailhead: Four trailheads allow access to the trail at various segments. They are located at Railroad Cave at Big Lake, Lightning Ridge, Sheeps Crossing, and Big Cienega. From Eagar, drive west on AZ 260 17 miles to Railroad Cove. There is parking for up to 10 vehicles. Toilets are provided.

WEST FORK TRAIL #94

Highlights: This is the first half (7 miles) of West Baldy Trail #94. This trail is not located in the Mt. Baldy Wilderness until it joins West Baldy Trail #94 at the 7-mile point.

Total Distance: 7 miles. Your ride can be lengthened via connecting trails.

Location: Mt. Baldy Wilderness and adjoining area

Type of Trail: Equestrian/Hiker/Mountain Bikes

Connecting Trails: West Baldy Trail #94, Sheeps Crossing Trail

Difficulty: Moderate

Elevation: 8,500 to 9,000 feet

Best Months: May through October

Maps: Apache-Sitgreaves National Forest USGS: 258SW Greer, AZ; NW Big Lake, AZ

Special Considerations: This is a relatively easy ride with level to short steep climbs. It parallels FR 87 in spots. Use caution crossing FR 87 because of traffic. When the trail comes to Sheeps Crossing, it enters the Mt. Baldy Wilderness.

Trailhead: The trail begins on Osborne Road in Greer, or FR 87.

WEST BALDY TRAIL #94

Highlights: A fun and easy ride with great panoramic views. This trail is the continuation of Trail #94 (West Fork), which begins in Greer (Osborne Road).

Total Distance: 14 miles. Your ride can be lengthened via connecting trails.

Location: Mt. Baldy Wilderness and adjoining area

Type of Trail: Equestrian/Hiker

Connecting Trails: West Fork Trail #94, Sheeps Crossing Trail

Difficulty: Easy

Elevation: 9,000 to 11,200 feet

Best Months: May through October

Maps: Apache-Sitgreaves National Forest USGS: 279NW Mt. Ord, AZ; 280NW Big Lake, AZ

Special Considerations: You may encounter snow as late as June. The Little Colorado River is home to several small colonies of beaver. Trout fishing can be good at times. Please sign in and out. The summit of Mount Baldy is located on the White Mountain Apache Indian Reservation, and is closed to non–tribe members.

Trailhead: From Pinetop, travel east on AZ 260. Turn right on FR 273 and proceed to Sheeps Crossing trailhead.

SOUTH FORK TRAIL #97

Highlights: A relatively easy and comfortable ride through beautiful country. Cool water with great views; the trail goes to Mexican Hay Lake.

Total Distance: 14 miles
Location: White Mountains
Type of Trail: Equestrian/Hiker/Mountain Biker
Difficulty: Easy
Elevation: 7,500 to 9,000 feet
Best Months: April through November
Maps: Apache-Sitgreaves National Forest USGS: 258SW Greer, AZ;
258SE Eagar, AZ
Special Considerations: The trail is for day use only. Water is available along the river for stock, fishing, or cooling your feet. The road to the trailhead at Mexican Hay Lake can be muddy. You may need to park by the gate and ride to the trailhead.
Trailhead: From Lakeside, travel east on AZ 260 to the sign for South Fork. Turn right on FR 4124. This road will open up into a beautiful canyon. Follow it to the campground and trailhead.

EAST BALDY TRAIL #95
(AKA PHELPS TRAIL OR EAST FORK TRAIL)

Highlights: A fun ride with great panoramic views. Meadows give way to sandstone, boulders, and conifers. The trail alternates between timber and bare rock. Seven miles from the trailhead, the trail merges with Sheeps Crossing Trail #94, which could allow you to shuttle the horses from one trailhead to another.
Total Distance: 14 miles. Your ride can be lengthened via connecting trails.
Location: Mt. Baldy Wilderness
Type of Trail: Equestrian/Hiker
Connecting Trails: Sheeps Crossing Trail #94
Difficulty: Moderate
Elevation: 9,300 to 11,200 feet
Best Months: May through October
Maps: Apache-Sitgreaves National Forest USGS: 279NE Mt. Ord, AZ; 280NW Big Lake, AZ
Special Considerations: You may encounter snow as late as June. The Little Colorado River is home to several small colonies of

beaver. Trout fishing can be good in the river. At Gabaldon Campground, there are five units with horse corrals, five rings, a vault, and toilets. Water at nearby stream. Please sign in. The summit of Mount Baldy is located on the White Mountain Apache Reservation, and is closed to non–tribe members.

Trailhead: Two trailheads, both located off AZ 273. Phelp's trailhead is on the north side of the East Fork of the Little Colorado River, and the second trailhead is at Gabaldon Campground.

Coconino National Forest

THE COCONINO NATIONAL FOREST is a land of great diversity. Three districts and unique land groups comprise this 1,821,495-acre forest. The most northern part is the volcanic highlands. The gems of the highlands are the San Francisco Peaks and 12,633-foot Mt. Humphreys. In the southern part are Desert Canyon and the red rock country, with lower elevation, warmer temperatures, and an arid environment. Much different are the grassy plateaus and the ponderosa pine forests of the Mogollon Rim and plateau country. The Mogollon Rim and plateau country are similar to each other, with average elevations of 7,000 feet, cooler temperatures, and four distinct seasons. Lake Mary, Arizona's largest natural lake, is found here.

The Coconino Forest has a long and interesting history. The first Europeans arrived in 1583 with the expedition of Spaniard Antonio de Espejo, who explored the Wet Beaver Creek and Verde River areas. Spanish expeditions to the area continued from 1596 to 1605.

The years 1605–1850 were marked by indifference, with little of interest for anyone except for the fur trading mountain men. However, in 1863, everything changed when gold was found in the Prescott area. Miners, prospectors, and farmers began to displace the Yavapai and Apache Indians, causing social disharmony and war. The mere presence of the militia exacerbated the Indian-White conflicts.

In 1872–1873, General George Crook, an Indian fighter, brought innovative techniques to control the Indians, one of which was better military supply. This required a reliable easy route to move supplies from Ft. Apache to Ft. Verde and Ft. Whipple. And so was born the General Crook Trail.

In 1861–1862, construction of the railroad began, particularly around Flagstaff and Williams, following a course initially set by the Beale Wagon Trail. Railroad development was initially slow because of labor shortages. Eventually, large group of Mormon workers came to work under the leadership of John W. Young, who built two work camps in Flagstaff and one just north of the city. The latter, at LeRoux Springs, had a stockaded village known as Ft. Moroni. Ft. Moroni was accidentally burned in 1920. The area's name was later changed from LeRoux Springs to Ft. Valley.

The single most important asset industry in northern Arizona was timber. The railroads and the economy could not, and would not, grow without it. As demand for timber grew, so did concern for the health and sanctity of the forests. The Forest Reserve Act of 1897 and the San Francisco and Black Mesa Forest Reserves were created to protect these beautiful northern Arizona woodlands.

In 1907 and 1908, these two reserves became the Coconino and Black Mesa National Forests, and in 1919, the two forests were combined into one, the Coconino National Forest. "Coconino" refers to the Hopi and Yavapai Indians. The national forest is so named for its central location in the Hopi and Yavapai Indian country.

Coconino National Forest Trails

Beaver Creek and Long Valley Ranger Districts

Coconino National Forest
Beaver Creek Ranger District
HC 64, Box 240
Rimrock, AZ 86335
928-567-4510

Coconino National Forest
Long Valley Ranger District
PO Box 68
Happy Jack, AZ 86024
928-354-2216

Nearby Cities
Flagstaff, Rimrock, Happy Jack

Peaks Ranger District

Coconino National Forest
Peaks Ranger District
3075 N Hwy 89
Flagstaff, AZ 86004
928-526-0866

Nearby City
Flagstaff

Page	Trails
58	Little Elden Trail
58	Heart Trail #103
59	Kachina Trail #150
59	Inner Basin Trail #29
60	Abineau and Bear Jaw Trails #127 and 26

Page	Trails
60	Wetherford Trail #102
61	Arizona Trail (Equestrian Bypass)
62	Arizona Trail (Marshall Lake to Fisher Point)

Sedona Ranger District

Coconino National Forest
Sedona Ranger District
PO Box 300
Sedona, AZ 86336
928-282-4119

Nearby Cities
Sedona, Flagstaff, Camp Verde, Strawberry, Cottonwood

Page	Trails
63	Hot Loop Trail #94
64	North Wilson Trail #123 and Wilson Mountain Trail #10
64	Loy Canyon Trail #5

Page	Trails
64	Jacks Canyon Trail #55
65	Mail Trail #84
65	Flume Road Trail #154
66	Towel Creek Trail #67
66	Walker Basin Trail #81

Blue Ridge Ranger District

Coconino National Forest
Blue Ridge Ranger District
HC 31 Box 300
Happy Jack, AZ 86024
928-477-2255

Nearby Cities
Happy Jack, Payson, Strawberry, Pine

Beaver Creek Ranger District

BELL TRAIL #13

Highlights: A popular well-developed route into Wet Beaver Creek Canyon. Trail's terminus is at FR 24.

Total Distance: 11 miles. Your ride can be lengthened via connecting trails.

Location: Wet Beaver Creek and West Clear Creek Wilderness

Type of Trail: Equestrian/Hiker

Connecting Trails: Long Canyon Trail #63, Apache Maid Trail #15

Difficulty: Moderate

Elevation: 4,000 to 6,400 feet

Best Months: Year-round

Maps: Coconino National Forest USGS: Casner Butte, Walker Mountain

Trailhead: From Flagstaff, drive south on I-17 40 miles to AZ 179 (exit 298). Turn east on AZ 179 and drive 115 miles to the Beaver Creek Ranger Station. Go north 0.25 mile to parking lot and trailhead.

LONG CANYON TRAIL #63

Highlights: The area through which the Long Canyon Trail meanders was once used by the Sinaqua Indians. Please do not disturb any artifacts you may encounter.

Total Distance: 9.5 miles. Your ride can be lengthened via connecting trails.

Location: Coconino National Forest, Mogollon Rim

Type of Trail: Equestrian/Hiker

Connecting Trails: Bell Trail #13

Difficulty: Difficult

Elevation: 3,700 to 5,700 feet

Best Months: April through November

Maps: Coconino National Forest USGS: Apache Maid Mountain, Casner Butte

Special Considerations: This trail starts upstream of the Beaver Creek Campground. Once the trail reaches the Mogollon Rim, it may become indistinct and hard to follow. Look for rock cairns that mark the trail.

Trailhead: From Flagstaff, drive south on I-17 40 miles to exit 298 (AZ 179). Turning east directs you to FR 618, which is on the east side of the underpass. Travel east on FR 618 about 2.5 miles to FR 618H, which is the first road past Beaver Creek. The trailhead is 0.75 mile ahead on the right side.

WEST CLEAR CREEK TRAIL #17

Highlights: Multiple creek crossings

Total Distance: 7.5 miles. Your ride can be lengthened via connecting trails.

Location: Clear Creek Wilderness

Type of Trail: Equestrian/Hiker

Connecting Trails: Blodgett Basin Trail (connects FR 214 to FR 215)

Difficulty: Easy to difficult

Elevation: 5,800 to 4,000 feet

Best Months: Year-round

Maps: Coconino National Forest USGS: Walker Mountain, Buckhorn Mountain

Special Considerations: At the trail's terminus at Bald Hill, the trail will drop 1,800 feet down a steep talus-strewn slope from the high plateau piñon-juniper forest to the canyon floor.

Trailhead: There are two access points: From Flagstaff, drive south on I-17 40 miles to exit 298 (AZ 179). Turning east directs you to FR 618, which is on the east side of the underpass. Travel east on FR 618 to FR 215, then turn east. Travel 3 miles to the Bullpen Ranch trailhead. Or, from I-17, travel east on FR 618 about 8 miles to FR 214. Turn east and travel 4.7 miles to Bald Hill Road. The trailhead is 1 mile ahead on this primitive road.

Beaver Creek and Long Valley Ranger Districts

APACHE MAID TRAIL #15

Highlights: A scenic trail through the rock gorges of the Colorado Plateau.

Total Distance: 13 miles. Your ride can be lengthened via connecting trails.

Location: West Clear Creek and Wet Beaver Creek Wilderness

Type of Trail: Equestrian/Hiker

Connecting Trails: Bell Trail #13

Difficulty: Moderate to difficult

Elevation: 3,700 to 6,500 feet

Best Months: April through November

Maps: Coconino National Forest USGS: Casner Butte

Trailhead: From Flagstaff, drive south on I-17 40 miles. Turn east on exit 298, AZ 179, and drive 1.5 miles to the Beaver Creek Ranger Station turnoff. The parking lot and trailhead are 0.25 mile north.

Peaks Ranger District

LITTLE ELDEN TRAIL

Highlights: Because of its use by mountain bikers, this trail is best used in concert with other trails. It also is used by local horseback riders.

Total Distance: 4.7 miles (one way). Your ride can be lengthened via connecting trails.

Location: San Francisco Peaks

Type of Trail: Equestrian/Hiker/Mountain Biker

Connecting Trails: Heart Trail #103, Sandy Seep Trail #129, Elden Lookout Trail #4, Sunset Trail #23, Brookbank Trail #2, Rocky Ridge Trail #153, Schultz Creek Trail #152

Difficulty: Easy

Elevation: 7,300 to 7,800 feet

Best Months: April through November

Maps: Coconino National Forest USGS: Sunset Crater West

Trailhead: From Flagstaff, travel north on US 89 to Elden Spring Road (FR 556). Turn left on Elden Spring Road (FR 556) and continue for 3.5 miles to the Little Elden trailhead on the right.

HEART TRAIL #103

Highlights: This trail passes through a large mixed-conifer forest, which was destroyed by the Radio fire in 1977. The area is now well into regeneration.

Total Distance: 3.5 miles. You can lengthen your ride via connecting trails.

Location: San Francisco Peaks

Type of Trail: Equestrian/Hiker/Mountain Bikers

Connecting Trails: Little Elden Trail, Sandy Seep Trail #129, Sunset Trail #23

Difficulty: Difficult

Elevation: 7,200 to 8,500 feet

Best Months: April through November

Maps: Coconino National Forest USGS: Sunset Crater West

Special Considerations: The best access is from the Sandy Seep trailhead.

Trailhead: From Flagstaff, travel north on US 89 about 1.5 miles past the Peaks Ranger Station. Just past the Elden Pueblo on the west side of the road is the trailhead.

KACHINA TRAIL #150

Highlights: An easy ride with a great view.

Total Distance: 5 miles. Your ride can be lengthened via connecting trails.

Location: San Francisco Peaks

Type of Trail: Equestrian/Hiker

Connecting Trails: Wetherford Trail #102

Difficulty: Moderate to easy

Elevation: 10,000 to 9,000 feet

Best Months: May through October

Maps: Coconino National Forest USGS: Humphreys Peak

Special Considerations: A fall ride offers great aspen color and bugling elk.

Trailhead: From Flagstaff, travel north on US 180 to FR 522 (Snow Bowl Road). Follow FR 522 to the Snow Bowl. The first parking lot is on the right. The trailhead is at the south end of the parking lot.

INNER BASIN TRAIL #29

Highlights: Great views. Superb aspen color in the fall. Snowfields may be present in summer. To protect the watershed do not enter the Inner Basin.

Total Distance: 6 miles

Location: Kachina Peaks Wilderness

Type of Trail: Equestrian/Hiker. Mountain bikers only in first portion of trail.

Difficulty: Moderate

Elevation: 8,600 to 10,150 feet

Best Months: May through October

Maps: Coconino National Forest USGS: Humphreys Peak Quad
Special Considerations: This volcanic mountain's side blew out with
the volcano, making this area similar to that of Mt. St. Helen's after
the cataclysmic event, which changed the mountain forever.
Trailhead: From Flagstaff, travel north on US 89 12.5 miles to
FR 552 (which is 1 mile past the Sunset Crater turnoff). Turn left
on FR 552, and travel 1 mile. Turn right at the Lockett Meadow
sign and continue to the trailhead.

ABINEAU AND BEAR JAW TRAILS #127 AND #26

Highlights: A loop trail with superb panoramic views. The Grand
Canyon is visible to the north.
Total Distance: 6 miles
Location: San Francisco Peaks Wilderness
Type of Trail: Equestrian/Hiker
Difficulty: Difficult
Elevation: 8,500 to 10,500 feet
Best Months: May through October
Maps: Coconino National Forest USGS: White Horse Hills,
Humphreys Peak Quad
Special Considerations: Snow may be encountered in late spring and
early fall.
Trailhead: From Flagstaff, travel north on US 89 14 miles. Turn left
on FR 418 and go 7 miles to FR 9123 (which is about 1 mile east of
Reese Tank). Travel south on FR 9123 1.2 miles to the trailhead.

WETHERFORD TRAIL #102

Highlights: Alpine terrain in the high peak area. Superb panoramic
views. Great aspen color in the fall.
Total Distance: 8.7 miles (one way)
Location: San Francisco Peaks Wilderness
Type of Trail: Equestrian/Hiker
Connecting Trails: Humphreys Trail, Kachina Trail #150
Difficulty: Moderate to difficult

Elevation: 8,800 to 12,000 feet
Best Months: May through October
Maps: Coconino National Forest USGS: Humphreys Peak
Special Considerations: Snow may be encountered in the spring or
early fall.
Trailhead: From Flagstaff, travel north on US 180 to FR 420 (Schultz
Pass Road). Turn right and travel to FR 557. Turn left to continue
on FR 420 for 6 miles to the trailhead at Schultz Tank.

ARIZONA TRAIL (EQUESTRIAN BYPASS)

Highlights: This trail gives the equestrian user a bypass around
Flagstaff.
Total Distance: 9 miles. Your ride can be lengthened via connecting
trails.
Location: Flagstaff
Type of Trail: Equestrian/Hiker
Connecting Trails: Fisher Point–Marshall Lake, Arizona Trail
segment
Difficulty: Moderate
Elevation: 6,750 to 7,100 feet
Best Months: Spring through fall
Maps: Coconino National Forest, Arizona Trail Map USGS:
Flagstaff East, Winona
Special Considerations: From the trailhead, you will have a choice
of north or south travel. Traveling north for 3.5 miles will bring
you out by I-40. If you travel south, you will follow the Walnut
Canyon Rim headed toward Marshall Lake, which is a more
desirable ride.
Trailhead: There are three access points. You may access from the
backcountry trail at Fisher Point, or from FR 301 (on Butler
Avenue) off FR 303 (from the Country Club). From Flagstaff,
take Country Club Drive to Oakmont Drive and turn left.
Oakmont Drive becomes FR 303. Continue on FR 303 for
3.8 miles to the trailhead, which is on the right (south) side of
the road.

ARIZONA TRAIL
(MARSHALL LAKE TO FISHER POINT)

Highlights: Good views and abundant wildlife.

Total Distance: 5.7 miles. Your ride can be lengthened via connecting trails.

Location: near Flagstaff

Type of Trail: Equestrian/Hiker/Mountain Biker

Connecting Trails: Arizona Trail segments

Difficulty: Moderate

Elevation: 7,050 to 6,750 feet

Best Months: Year-round

Maps: Coconino National Forest, Arizona Trail Map USGS: Flagstaff East

Special Considerations: This is a nonmotorized multiple-use trail, so you may encounter some mountain bikers. You may encounter snow in the winter.

Trailhead: There are two access points for this trail, both east of Flagstaff and off Lake Mary Road. To access Fisher Point, use the Sandy's Canyon trailhead. Take Lake Mary Road (FR 3) south and east from Flagstaff. At 6 miles from Flagstaff, at the second cattle guard, either turn left (north) to the trailhead or continue about 4 miles farther to the Marshall Lake turnoff. Follow the signs to Marshall Lake and the trailhead.

Sedona Ranger District

HOT LOOP TRAIL #94

Highlights: Panoramic views and impressive views of red rocks.
Total Distance: 10.2 miles (one way). Your ride can be lengthened via connecting trails.
Location: Munds Mountain Wilderness
Type of Trail: Equestrian/Hiker
Connecting Trails: Munds Mountain Trail #77, Jacks Canyon Trail #55
Difficulty: Moderate to difficult
Elevation: 4,200 to 6,200 feet
Best Months: Year-round
Maps: Coconino National Forest USGS: Munds Mountain
Special Considerations: The trail may be hard to find as a footpath, but follow rock cairns. The stream in Woods Canyon can be a torrent during spring snowmelt or summer thunderstorms.
Trailhead: From Flagstaff, drive 30 miles south on US 89A to Sedona. Turn left onto AZ 179 and drive 7.3 miles to FR 793 (Jacks Canyon Road). Turn left and continue 3 miles to the trailhead.

NORTH WILSON TRAIL #123 AND WILSON MOUNTAIN TRAIL #10

Highlights: Just north of Midgely Bridge in the parking lot is a monument to Richard Wilson, who was killed by a grizzly bear in 1885.
Total Distance: 5.6 miles
Location: Munds Mountain Wilderness
Type of Trail: Equestrian/Hiker
Connecting Trails: Wilson Mountain Trail #10, which connects to North Wilson Trail #123.
Difficulty: Difficult
Elevation: 4,600 to 7,900 feet
Best Months: April through November
Maps: Coconino National Forest USGS: Wilson Mountain Munds Park

Special Considerations: North Wilson Trail #123 is cooler in summer than Wilson Mountain Trail #10.

Trailhead: From Flagstaff, drive south on US 89A 22 miles. The trailhead is just north of Midgely Bridge.

LOY CANYON TRAIL #5

Highlights: A historical trail used by the Samuel Coy family in the 1880s to move livestock to and from summer pasture.

Total Distance: 5 miles

Location: Munds Mountain Wilderness

Type of Trail: Equestrian/Hiker

Difficulty: Easy to difficult

Elevation: 4,720 to 6,500 feet

Best Months: Year-round

Maps: Coconino National Forest USGS: Coy Butte

Trailhead: From Flagstaff, drive south on US 89A 35 miles. At 5 miles south of Sedona turn north on FR 525. Follow the signs 9.3 miles to Coy Butte. The parking lot is on the left prior to crossing the cattle guard to the Hancock Ranch.

JACKS CANYON TRAIL #55

Highlights: Great panoramic view of the red rock country from the summit of Munds Mountain.

Total Distance: 5.7 miles. Your ride can be lengthened via connecting trails.

Location: Munds Mountain Wilderness

Type of Trail: Equestrian/Hiker

Connecting Trails: Munds Mountain Trail, Hot Loop Trail #94

Difficulty: Moderate to difficult

Elevation: 4,200 to 6,300 feet

Best Months: March through November

Maps: Coconino National Forest USGS: Munds Mountain

Trailhead: From Flagstaff, drive south on US 89A 30 miles to AZ 179 in Sedona. Turn left at the traffic light and drive 7.3 miles to FR 793 (Jacks Canyon Road). Turn left and continue 3 miles to the trailhead.

MAIL TRAIL #84

Highlights: A pleasant ride into the historic Fossil Springs area.

Total Distance: 3.1 miles. Your ride can be lengthened via connecting trails.

Location: Fossil Springs Wilderness

Type of Trail: Equestrian/Hiker

Connecting Trails: Fossil Springs Trail #118

Difficulty: Moderate

Elevation: 4,300 to 5,600 feet

Best Months: Year-round

Maps: Coconino National Forest USGS: Strawberry

Special Considerations: On the access road, four-wheel-drive and high-clearance vehicles are recommended. Wet weather may make this road impossible.

Trailhead: From Camp Verde, proceed east on AZ 260 (General Crook Trail). Drive 13 miles past the bridge over West Clear Creek, then turn right onto FR 9247B. Follow this road as it parallels the power line. Turn left on the road just past the cattle guard and continue to the parking area near the stock tank.

FLUME ROAD TRAIL #154

Highlights: A historic road that was used to move materials for construction of the Irving Power Plant.

Total Distance: 3.5 miles

Location: Fossil Springs Wilderness Area

Type of Trail: Equestrian/Hiker

Difficulty: Easy

Elevation: 3,800 to 4,240 feet

Best Months: Year-round

Maps: Coconino National Forest USGS: Strawberry

Trailhead: There are two access points. From Camp Verde, travel on AZ 260 to FR 708. Turn south on FR 708 and drive about 20 miles to the trailhead. Or, from Strawberry, drive on AZ 87. Turn west onto FR 708 and proceed 14 miles to the trailhead.

TOWEL CREEK TRAIL #67

Highlights: This interesting trail is used to move cattle to and from
   seasonal range. Towel Spring Spur (3 miles in) passes the Old Line
   Cabin, still in use by cowboys. Access to the Verde River.
Total Distance: 6.4 miles
Location: Fossil Springs Wilderness
Type of Trail: Equestrian/Hiker
Difficulty: Moderate
Elevation: 4,100 to 3,000 feet
Best Months: Year-round
Maps: Coconino National Forest USGS: Hackberry Mountain,
   Horner Mountain
Trailhead: From Flagstaff, travel south on I-17 about 50 miles and
   get off at the Middle Verde exit. Drive east on FR 9 through Camp
   Verde (the General Crook Highway) about 6 miles to FR 708.
   Turn southeast on FR 708 and proceed 9 miles to the trailhead
   near Needle Rock.

WALKER BASIN TRAIL #81

Highlights: Panoramic views of a classic western landscape.
Total Distance: 8 miles
Location: Beaver Creek
Type of Trail: Equestrian/Hiker
Difficulty: Moderate
Elevation: 4,000 to 6,000 feet
Best Months: Year-round
Maps: Coconino National Forest USGS: Walker Mountain
Special Considerations: Rock cairns may mark the trail. May be hot
   in the summer.
Trailhead: From Flagstaff, drive south on I-17 40 miles. Exit at
   AZ 179 (east). Turn on FR 618 and go about 9 miles. Turn east
   on FR 214 and drive 7.3 miles to the trailhead where the Jeep
   track turns off to the left.

Blue Ridge Ranger District

BARBERSHOP TRAIL #91

Highlights: Great fall colors.
Total Distance: 4.5 miles. Your ride can be lengthened via connecting trails.
Location: Mogollon Rim
Type of Trail: Equestrian/Hiker
Connecting Trails: Houston Brothers Trail #18 via U-Bar Trail #28 (6.5 miles)
Difficulty: Moderate
Elevation: 7,600 to 7,300 feet
Best Months: April through November
Maps: Coconino National Forest USGS: Dane Canyon
Special Considerations: Water is available on the trail.
Trailhead: From Payson, travel north on AZ 87 to FR 95 and turn south. Travel 8 miles to FR 139. Turn right and continue on FR 139 to the trailhead.

HOUSTON BROTHERS TRAIL #18

Highlights: A historic trail that meanders along the floor of Houston Draw. There is a spring-fed perennial stream. This trail is part of the Cabin Loop Trail.
Total Distance: 7 miles. Your ride can be lengthened via connecting trails.
Location: Mogollon Rim
Type of Trail: Equestrian/Hiker
Connecting Trails: Fred Haught System Trail #22, Barbershop Trail #91 via U-Bar Trail #28 (6.5 miles)
Difficulty: Moderate
Elevation: 6,900 to 7,600 feet
Best Months: April through November
Maps: Coconino National Forest USGS: Blue Ridge Reservoir, Dane Canyon

Special Considerations: The trailhead is near the Gifford Pinchot
   Cabin. Gifford Pinchot is considered the father of the National Forest
   Service, and his cabin site has been singled out for its serene beauty.
Trailhead: From Payson, drive north on AZ 87 about 30 miles.
   Turn south on FR 95 and travel 8 miles to FR 139A. Turn left on
   FR 139A and travel 7 miles to the trailhead near Pinchot Cabin.

U-BAR TRAIL #28

Highlights: This trail is part of the Cabin Loop Trail, a main connec-
   tor between Houston Brothers Trail #18 and Barbershop Trail #91.
Total Distance: 6.5 miles. Your ride can be lengthened via connecting
   trails.
Location: Mogollon Rim
Type of Trail: Equestrian/Hiker
Connecting Trails: Fred Haught System Trail #22, Barbershop Trail
   #91 to Houston Brothers Trail #18 via U-Bar Trail #28
Difficulty: Moderate
Elevation: 6,900 to 7,600 feet
Best Months: April through November
Maps: Coconino National Forest USGS: Blue Ridge Reservoir, Dane
   Canyon
Special Considerations: This is a backcountry access trail reached only
   from Barbershop Trail #91 or Houston Brothers Trail #18. Sections of
   the trail are not clearly marked; you will need to follow blazes.
Trailhead: There are two access points: For Houston Brothers Trail #18,
   from Payson, drive north on AZ 87 to FR 95. Turn south and travel
   8 miles to FR 139A. Turn left on FR 139 and travel 7 miles to the
   trailhead near Pinchot Cabin. For Barbershop Trail #91, from Payson,
   drive north on AZ 87 to FR 95 and turn south. Travel 8 miles to
   FR 139. Turn right (south) and continue on FR 139 to the trailhead.

FRED HAUGHT TRAIL #22

Highlights: This historic Trail is part of the Cabin Loop Trail. It was
   named after a local rancher. Scenic views from Mogollon Rim.
   Abundant wildlife.

Total Distance: 6 miles. Your ride can be lengthened via connecting trails.
Location: Mogollon Rim
Type of Trail: Equestrian/Hiker
Connecting Trails: Houston Brothers Trail #18, Barbershop Trail #91, U-Bar Trail #28
Difficulty: Moderate
Elevation: 6,900 to 7,300 feet
Best Months: April through November
Maps: Coconino National Forest USGS: Blue Ridge Reservoir, Dane County
Special Considerations: Water is generally available on this trail.
Trailhead: From Payson, drive north on AZ 87 about 30 miles to FR 95. Turn south and travel 8 miles to FR 139. Turn left on FR 139 and proceed to the trailhead.

GENERAL CROOK TRAIL #130

Highlights: A historic trail named after and built under the command of General George Crook. Originally 200 but now 138 miles long, it passes along the Mogollon Rim and through the jurisdiction of three national forests. The trail was originally built to provide a supply route from Ft. Whipple (near Prescott), to Ft. Apache (in White River).
Total Distance: 25 miles
Location: Mogollon Rim
Type of Trail: Equestrian/Hiker
Connecting Trails: Fred Haught Trail #22, Houston Brothers Trail #18, Barbershop Trail #91
Difficulty: Easy
Elevation: 7,900 to 7,000 feet
Best Months: Year-round
Maps: Coconino National Forest Service Map. USGS: Dane Canyon
Trailhead: From Flagstaff drive south on 55 miles on FR 3 (Lake Mary Road). Turn right (south) on AZ 87 and drive 9 miles to FR 300. You will find multiple access points along this road.

Blue Ridge Segment of Arizona Trail

Highlights: A pleasant trail through meadows, forest, and canyons.
Total Distance: 8 miles
Location: Mogollon Rim
Type of Trail: Equestrian/Hiker
Difficulty: Moderate
Elevation: 6,900 to 7,300 feet
Best Months: Spring through fall
Maps: Coconino National Forest Service, Arizona Trail Map USGS: Dane Canyon, Blue Ridge Reservoir
Trailhead: From Flagstaff, drive east and south on Lake Mary Road to Clint's Well, located on AZ 87. Turn right (south) on AZ 87 and drive 9 miles to FR 300 (General Crook Trail). Turn east on FR 300 and drive 6 miles to the General Springs trailhead, or turn north from Clint's Well on AZ 87 and drive 7.5 miles to the Blue Ridge trailhead. This trailhead is also accessible from Payson by driving north on AZ 87, or from the east by driving on AZ 260.

Coronado National Forest

THE CORONADO NATIONAL FOREST is a 1,780,000-acre jewel in southern Arizona. It is composed of twelve mountain ranges or "sky islands" and eight wilderness areas and national monuments. The forest areas range from the U.S.-Mexico border on the south to the Arizona–New Mexico line on the east. Elevation ranges from 3,000 feet to the 9,797-foot summit of Chiricahua Peak and the 10,720-foot Mt. Graham. Parker Canyon Lake and Riggs Lake are both fishing lakes.

Several Indian cultures inhabited this area prior to exploration by the Franciscans and Jesuits. Friar Marces de Niza and companion Esteban's claims of gold and riches in the seven cities of Cibola brought exploration by Don Francisco Vásquez de Coronado. In the late 1600s, the Jesuits and Franciscans returned, followed by prospectors in search of gold and silver. The threat these Europeans placed on the natives, particularly the Apaches, created cultural clashes that brought notoriety to the Apache leaders Cochise and Geronimo.

Coronado National Forest Trails

Douglas Ranger District
Coronado National Forest
Douglas Ranger District
3081 N. Leslie Canyon Road
Douglas, AZ 85607
520-364-3468

Nearby Cities
Douglas, Tucson, Benson

Nogales Ranger District
Coronado National Forest
Nogales Ranger District
303 Old Tucson Road
Nogales, AZ 85621
520-281-2296

Nearby City
Nogales

Sierra Vista Ranger District
Coronado National Forest
Sierra Vista Ranger District
5990 S. Highway 92
Hereford, AZ 85615
520-378-0311

Nearby City
Sierra Vista

Safford Ranger District
Coronado National Forest
Safford Ranger District
PO Box 709
Safford, AZ 85348-0709
520-428-4150

Nearby Cities
Safford, Bonita

Santa Catalina Ranger District
Coronado National Forest
Santa Catalina Ranger District
5700 N. Sabino Canyon Road
Tucson, AZ 85715
520-749-8700

Nearby City
Tucson

Douglas Ranger District

BASIN TRAIL #600

Highlights: A short steep trail used as a connector to the Greenhouse Trail and Ash Spring Trail out of the Herb Martyr Campground.
Total Distance: 2.8 miles. Your ride can be lengthened via connecting trails.
Location: Chiricahua Mountain Wilderness
Type of Trail: Equestrian/Hiker
Connecting Trails: Greenhouse Trail #248, Ash Spring Trail #247A via FR 713
Difficulty: Difficult
Elevation: 6,240 to 9,240 feet
Best Months: Spring through fall
Maps: Coronado National Forest USGS: Chiricahua Peak, Portal, Rustler Park
Special Considerations: FR 42 is usually closed after snowstorms and can be muddy and slick after a rainstorm.
Trailhead: From Tucson, drive east on I-10 139 miles to US 80. (You will briefly cross into New Mexico.) Turn right (south), and travel on US 80 for about 28 miles. Turn right (west) on Portal Road and drive 7 miles. Turn west on FR 42 and travel about 4 miles to FR 42A. Turn left (west), and continue 2 miles farther to FR 713, a four-wheel-drive road. The trailhead is located near the end of the road.

MONTE VISTA TRAIL #221

Highlights: Outstanding views. Access to the Crest Trail. Can be a loop trail.
Total Distance: 4.6 miles. Your ride can be lengthened or looped via connecting trails.
Location: Chiricahua Mountain Wilderness
Type of Trail: Equestrian/Hiker
Connecting Trails: Crest Trail #270, and multiple other trails that connect with it.

Difficulty: Difficult

Elevation: 6,100 to 9,357 feet

Best Months: Spring through fall

Maps: Coronado National Forest USGS: Chiricahua Peak

Special Considerations: To get to the summit, use the well-defined 0.2-mile spur.

Trailhead: There are multiple access points for this trail. From Tucson, travel east on I-10 72 miles to US 191. Turn right and drive south 29 miles to the Rucker Lake turnoff. Turn left (east) and drive 17 miles to the forest boundary. Continue on FR 74 for 5 miles to FR 74E. Turn left (north) on FR 74E and travel about 5 miles to the North Fork Canyon turnoff (FR 628). Turn left on FR 628. The trailhead is 2.8 miles further ahead. From Douglas, travel north on Leslie Canyon Road to Rucker Canyon. Stay on the main road, which becomes FR 74. Follow Douglas Road (FR 74) 45 miles. FR 74E becomes visible on the left. Turn left (north) on FR 74E and drive about 5 miles to the North Fork Canyon turnoff (FR 628). Turn left on FR 628; the trailhead is 2.8 miles down the road. Rucker Lake Road (FR 628) is a four-wheel-drive road, so you may want to continue on FR 47E to the trailhead at Rucker Forest Camp.

RASPBERRY RIDGE TRAIL #228

Highlights: Outstanding views. Access to the Crest Trail and a vast network of connecting trails.

Total Distance: 4.6 miles. Your ride can be lengthened via connecting trails.

Location: Chiricahua Mountain Wilderness

Type of Trail: Equestrian/Hiker

Connecting Trails: Crest Trail #270 and a multitude of trails that connect with it.

Difficulty: Difficult

Elevation: 6,100 to 9,357 feet

Best Months: Spring through fall

Maps: Coronado National Forest USGS: Chiricahua Peak

Special Considerations: Water can usually be found at Bear Springs. The Forest Service recommends walking your horse on the "razor-back" portion of this trail. Livestock are not permitted in the campground.

Trailhead: From Tucson, travel east on I-10 72 miles to US 191. Turn right and drive south 29 miles to the Rucker Lake turnoff. Turn left (east) and drive 17 miles to the forest boundary. Continue on FR 74 for 5 miles to FR 74E. Turn left and continue on 74E to the end of Rucker Forest Camp. Trailhead parking is available at the north end of the campground. From Douglas, travel north on Leslie Canyon Road to Rucker Canyon. Stay on the main road, which becomes FR 74. Follow Douglas Road (FR 74) for 45 miles. FR 74E becomes visible on the left. Turn left (north) on FR 74E about 5 miles to the North Fork Canyon turnoff (FR 628). Drive past the turnoff and continue on FR 74E to the end of Rucker Forest Camp. Trailhead parking is available at the north end of the campground.

GREENHOUSE TRAIL #248

Highlights: Access to the 400-foot Winn Falls and the Crest Trail #270. Access to the perennial Cima Creek.

Total Distance: 4.1 miles. Your ride can be lengthened via connecting trails.

Location: Chiricahua Mountain Wilderness

Type of Trail: Equestrian/Hiker

Connecting Trails: Crest Trail #270, Basin Trail #600

Difficulty: Difficult

Elevation: 6,240 to 9,240 feet

Best Months: Spring through fall

Maps: Coronado National Forest USGS: Chiricahua Peak, Portal, Rustler Park

Special Considerations: Your ride will be embellished by the historic cabins and idyllic setting around Cima Creek. The terminus of this trail is a 1,600-foot climb to its junction with Crest Trail #270. FR 42 is usually closed after snowstorms and can be muddy and slick after a rain.

Trailhead: From Tucson, drive east on I-10 139 miles to US 80. (You will briefly cross into New Mexico.) Turn right (south), and travel on US 80 about 28 miles. Turn right (west) on the Portal Road, and drive 7 miles. Turn west on FR 42 and travel about 4 miles to FR 42A. Turn left (west) and continue 2 miles to FR 713, a four-wheel-drive road. The trailhead is located near the end of the road.

CREST TRAIL #270 (BARFOOT LOOKOUT TO WILDERNESS BOUNDARY)

Highlights: The longest trail in the Chiricahua Mountains. Great views.

Total Distance: 4 miles. Your ride can be lengthened via connecting trails.

Location: Chiricahua Wilderness

Type of Trail: Equestrian/Hiker

Connecting Trails: Other portions of Crest Trail #270

Difficulty: Difficult

Elevation: 8,100 to 9,100 feet

Best Months: Spring through fall

Maps: Coronado National Forest USGS: Rustler Park

Trailhead: From Tucson, travel east on I-10 for 81 miles. Turn right (south) on AZ 186 and continue 4 miles toward Chiricahua National Monument. Turn right (south) on FR 42 and continue 12 miles toward Pinery Canyon to FR 42D. Turn right and drive about 2.5 miles to the Rustler Park Campground. The main access to this trail is via the Barfoot Lookout to the Wilderness boundary. The trailhead is on the west side of the campground near site #6.

CREST TRAIL #270 (WILDERNESS BOUNDARY TO MONTE VISTA LOOKOUT)

Highlights: Multiple connecting trails.

Total Distance: 6.3 miles. Your ride can be lengthened via connecting trails.

Location: Chiricahua Wilderness

Type of Trail: Equestrian/Hiker
Connecting Trails: Raspberry Ridge Trail #228, other portions of the
  Crest Trail
Difficulty: Easy
Elevation: 8,500 to 9,600 feet
Best Months: Spring through fall
Maps: Coronado National Forest USGS: Chiricahua Peak, Rustler
  Park
Trailhead: From Tucson, travel east on I-10 for 81 miles. Turn right
  (south) on AZ 186 and continue 4 miles toward Chiricahua
  National Monument. Turn right (south) on FR 42 and continue
  1.2 miles toward Pinery Canyon to FR 42D. Turn right and drive
  about 2.5 miles to the Rustler Park Campground. The main access
  to this trail is via the Barfoot Lookout to the Wilderness boundary.
  The trailhead is on the west side of the campground near site #6.

CREST TRAIL #270
(JUNCTION SADDLE TO SENTINEL PEAK)

Highlights: Multiple connecting trails, 9,000-foot summit.
Total Distance: 5.5 miles. Your ride can be lengthened via connecting
  trails.
Location: Chiricahua Mountain Wilderness
Type of Trail: Equestrian/Hiker
Connecting Trails: Price Canyon Trail #224, other portions of the
  Crest Trail
Difficulty: Easy
Elevation: 8,500 to 9,600 feet
Best Months: Spring through fall
Maps: Coronado National Forest USGS: Chiricahua Peak, Rustler
  Park
Special Considerations: No saddle horses or packhorses are allowed
  in the campground area.
Trailhead: None, as this part of the trail is accessible only from back-
  country trails. From Tucson, travel east on I-10 for 81 miles. Turn
  right (south) on AZ 186 and continue 4 miles toward the Chiricahua

National Monument. Turn right (south) on FR 42 and continue
12 miles toward Pinery Canyon to FR 42D. Turn right and drive
about 2.5 miles to the Rustler Park Campground. The main access
to this trail is via the Barfoot Lookout to the Wilderness boundary.
The trailhead is on the west side of the campground near site #6.

RED ROCK CANYON TRAIL #223

Highlights: A beautiful ride through a colorful canyon. Riparian
areas and forests. A loop trail when combined with other trails.
Total Distance: 4.9 miles. Your ride can be lengthened via connecting
trails.
Location: Chiricahua Mountain Wilderness
Type of Trail: Equestrian/Hiker
Connecting Trails: Price Canyon Trail #224, Crest Trail #270
Difficulty: Difficult
Elevation: 6,800 to 8,260 feet
Best Months: Year-round
Maps: Coronado National Forest USGS: Chiricahua Peak
Trailhead: From Douglas, take the Leslie Canyon Road north to
Rucker Canyon. Continue on this road, which becomes FR 74.
Continue to the junction of FR 74E. Turn left on FR 74E and
drive 3 miles to a primitive four-wheel-drive road (FR 4242).
You may wish to ride from here. If not, park your horse trailer
along FR 628.

RUCKER TRAIL #222

Highlights: A beautiful ride through colorful canyons. Riparian areas
and forests. A loop trail when combined with other trails.
Total Distance: 4.6 miles. Your ride can be lengthened via connecting
trails.
Location: Chiricahua Mountain Wilderness
Type of Trail: Equestrian/Hiker
Connecting Trails: Price Canyon Trail #224, Crest Trail #270
Difficulty: Difficult

Elevation: 6,800 to 8,260 feet

Best Months: Year-round

Maps: Coronado National Forest USGS: Chiricahua Peak

Special Considerations: You can also create a loop trail by riding
4.5 miles on FR 74E and FR 4242.

Trailhead: From Douglas, travel north on the Leslie Canyon Road
to Rucker Canyon. Continue on this road, which becomes FR 74.
Turn left (north) on FR 74E and drive 4.7 miles to Rucker Forest
Camp. The trailhead is at the end of this road.

MIDDLEMARCH CANYON TRAIL #277

Highlights: Remote and secluded. A connecting spur to Cochise
Trail #279.

Total Distance: 2.3 miles. Your ride can be lengthened via connecting
trails.

Location: Dragoon Mountains

Type of Trail: Equestrian/Hiker

Connecting Trails: Cochise Trail #279

Difficulty: Difficult

Elevation: 5,200 to 5,500 feet

Best Months: Spring through fall

Maps: Coronado National Forest USGS: Cochise, Stronghold

Special Considerations: Water is not available. This area can be very
hot.

Trailhead: From Tucson, travel east on I-10 for 72 miles to US 191.
Turn right (south) and drive 13 miles to Middlemarch Road
(FR 345); this road is on the east side of the Dragoon Mountains.
Turn right and drive 7 miles to FR 4388, a four-wheel-drive road.
Turn left and continue to the trailhead.

BOOTLEGGER TRAIL #257

Highlights: A beautiful forested connecting trail that can be looped
into Crest Trail #270. It is very steep. Do not connect into the poor
conditioned Rattlesnake Trail #275.

Total Distance: 1.6 miles. Your ride can be lengthened via connecting trails.
Location: Chiricahua Mountains
Type of Trail: Equestrian/Hiker
Connecting Trails: Crest Trail #270
Difficulty: Difficult
Elevation: 8,320 to 8,800 feet
Best Months: Spring through fall
Maps: Coronado National Forest USGS: Rustler Park
Special Considerations: This spur trail is for experienced riders and trail horses only. Pack and saddle stock are not allowed to overnight in the campground.
Trailhead: From Tucson, travel east on I-10 for 81 miles. Turn right (south) on AZ 186 and travel 23 miles. Turn left (east) on AZ 181 and travel 4 miles toward Chiricahua National Monument. Turn right (south) on FR 42. Continue 12 miles toward Pinery Canyon. Turn right on FR 42D and drive about 2.5 miles to the Rustler Park Campground. Ride down the Crest Trail 0.4 mile to the Bootlegger Trail. FR 42 and FR 42D are closed November through April and are slippery after a rain.

COCHISE TRAIL #279

Highlights: This historic trail leads into the Dragoon Mountain refuge of Cochise and his Chiricahua Apache tribe and extends from Cochise Stronghold Campground into West Stronghold Canyon of the Dragoon Mountains.
Total Distance: 4.5 miles. Your ride can be lengthened via connecting trails.
Location: Dragoon Mountains, Chiricahua Mountains
Type of Trail: Equestrian/Hiker
Connecting Trails: Show Tank Trail #281, Middlemarch Canyon Trail #277
Difficulty: Difficult
Elevation: 5,000 to 6,000 feet
Best Months: Spring through fall

Maps: Coronado National Forest USGS: Cochise Stronghold

Special Considerations: Water is available at the trailhead, but not along the trail. There is a camping area (unimproved) opposite the trailhead.

Trailhead: There are 2 access points to this trail. From Tucson, travel east on I-10 72 miles to US 191 (Dragoon Road, exit 318). Turn right (south) on US 191, and travel south about 11 miles to Ironwood. Turn right (near milepost 46) on Ironwood Road, and drive 8 miles to the Cochise Stronghold Campground. Equestrian trail users are asked to park at the first trailhead, which is located before the campground. From Benson, travel south on US 80. Turn left on the Middlemarch Road, 1 mile north of Tombstone. From the Middlemarch Road at the forest boundary, turn left onto FR 687 and proceed to the intersection of FR 688, a four-wheel-drive road. Turn right and drive to the trailhead at the end of the road. Also see page 81, Middlemarch Trail #277, for access to this trail midway.

Nogales Ranger District

SUPER TRAIL #134

Highlights: An easy loop trail to the 9,543-foot summit of Mt. Wrightson. This is a National Recreation Trail.

Total Distance: 8.1 miles. Your ride can be lengthened via connecting trails.

Location: Mt. Wrightson Wilderness, Santa Rita Mountains

Type of Trail: Equestrian/Hiker

Connecting Trails: Crest Trail #144 to the summit, Old Baldy Trail #372

Difficulty: Easy

Elevation: 5,400 to 9,450 feet

Best Months: Year-round

Maps: Coronado National Forest USGS: Mt. Wrightson

Special Considerations: This is a figure-eight trail, which can be combined with Old Baldy Trail #372.

Trailhead: From Tucson, travel south on I-19 to the Continental Road exit. Turn left (east) and proceed to the second four-way stop sign (Madera Canyon). Follow the signs to Madera Canyon and go about 13 miles to the trailhead.

OLD BALDY TRAIL #372

Highlights: A National Recreation Trail to the summit of 9,543-foot Mt. Wrightson, the highest peak in the Santa Ritas.

Total Distance: 4.5 miles. Your ride can be lengthened via connecting trails.

Location: Mt. Wrightson Wilderness, Santa Rita Mountains

Type of Trail: Equestrian/Hiker

Connecting Trails: Crest Trail #144 to the summit

Difficulty: Moderate

Elevation: 5,400 to 9,450 feet

Best Months: Year-round

Maps: Coronado National Forest USGS: Mt. Wrightson

Special Considerations: This trail is somewhat cooler in the summer, thanks to the north-side ascent of Mt. Wrightson. This is a figure-eight trail, which can be combined with the Super Trail.

Trailhead: From Tucson, travel south on I-19 to the Continental Road exit. Turn left (east) and proceed to the second four-way stop sign (Madera Canyon). Follow the signs to Madera Canyon and go about 13 miles to the trailhead.

FLORIDA CANYON TRAIL #145

Highlights: Wilderness canyon. Multiple connecting trails. Large stands of uncrowned Douglas fir. Access to the Santa Rita range.

Total Distance: 4.6 miles. Your ride can be lengthened via connecting trails.

Location: Mt. Wrightson Wilderness

Type of Trail: Equestrian/Hiker

Connecting Trails: Crest Trail #144, Cave Canyon Trail #149, Old Baldy Trail #372, Super Trail #134

Difficulty: Difficult

Elevation: 4,340 to 7,800 feet

Best Months: Spring through fall

Maps: Coronado National Forest USGS: Mt. Wrightson

Trailhead: From Tucson, drive south on I-19 and get off at Continental (exit 63). Turn east and follow the signs to Madera Canyon, about 7.3 miles to the FR 62 cutoff. Bear right onto FR 62A, and continue 3.6 miles to the Florida Canyon trailhead on the left, just outside the entrance to the Florida Work Center.

CREST TRAIL #144

Highlights: Outstanding vistas all along this trail to the summit of Mt. Wrightson.

Total Distance: 3.2 miles. Your ride can be lengthened via connecting trails.

Location: Mt. Wrightson Wilderness, Santa Rita Mountains

Type of Trail: Equestrian/Hiker

Connecting Trails: Florida Canyon Trail #145, Old Baldy Trail #372, Super Trail #134

Difficulty: Difficult

Elevation: 7,810 to 9,453 feet

Best Months: Spring through fall

Maps: Coronado National Forest USGS: Mt. Wrightson

Special Considerations: Near the summit are many short trails that connect with this trail.

Trailhead: This trail has backcountry access only. The best access is via Florida Canyon Trail #145. From Tucson, travel south on I-19 to the Continental exit (Madera Canyon Road). Turn east and follow the Madera Canyon Road about 7.3 miles to the FR 62 cutoff. Immediately bear right onto FR 62A, and follow this road about 3.6 miles. The Florida Canyon trailhead is on the left, just outside the Florida Work Area. Travel the Florida Canyon Trail for 4.6 miles to the Crest Trail.

Sierra Vista Ranger District

HUACHUCA MOUNTAIN PASSAGE (U.S.-MEXICO BORDER TO PARKER CANYON LAKE)

Highlights: The southernmost section of the Arizona Trail. It links the Coronado National Memorial (eventually the U.S.-Mexico border) to Parker Canyon Lake.

Total Distance: 20 miles. Your ride can be lengthened via connecting trails.

Location: Miller Peak Wilderness

Type of Trail: Equestrian/Hiker

Connecting Trails: Crest Trail #103, Sunnyside Canyon Trail #117 (See page 88, Crest Trail #103, for other connecting trails.)

Difficulty: Difficult

Elevation: 5,900 to 9,100 feet

Best Months: Year-round

Maps: Coronado National Forest USGS: Montezuma Pass, Miller Peak, Huachuca Peak

Special Considerations: Horses are not allowed on the Yaqui Ridge Trail or the Joe's Canyon Trail.

Trailhead: There are two access points for this trail. From Sierra Vista, drive south on AZ 92 13 miles to the Coronado National Memorial Road. Turn right and travel south 8.2 miles. Proceed through the Coronado National Memorial to the top of Montezuma Pass. The trailhead is across the road from the parking lot. For access from Tucson, travel east on I-10 to SR 83 (exit 281). Turn south and travel 50 miles through Sonoita to Parker Canyon Lake. Turn left on FR 48, and right on the South Lake Road (FR 194) to the trailhead.

CANELO HILLS PASSAGE #125 AND #131 (PARKER CANYON LAKE TO PATAGONIA)

Highlights: Part of the Arizona Trail, this trail links the Huachuca Mountains with the Canelo Hills and Patagonia and the South Rita Mountains.

Total Distance: 30.2 miles (Canelo Hills East #125 16.2 miles, Canelo Hills West #131 14 miles). Your ride can be lengthened via connecting trails.

Location: Huachuca Mountains, South Rita Mountains

Type of Trail: Equestrian/Hike

Connecting Trails: Scotia Canyon Trail #127

Difficulty: Moderate

Elevation: 4,000 to 5,400 feet

Best Months: Year-round

Maps: Coronado National Forest USGS: Mt. Hughes, O'Donnell Canyon, Canelo Pass, Huachuca Peak

Trailhead: There are 3 access points to this segment of the Arizona Trail. For the southern one, from Sonoita, travel south on AZ 83. About 0.5 mile prior to Parker Canyon Lake, turn south on FR 48 and travel 0.5 mile to FR 194 (South Lake Road). Turn right and follow FR 194 for 0.5 mile to the trailhead. For access to the Canelo Pass trailhead, from Sonoita, travel south on AZ 83 and turn south onto FR 799. (This is close to Canelo.) Travel 4 miles on FR 799 to the trailhead on the west side of the highway. For the north access, travel southwest on AZ 82 to FR 58 (which begins in front of the Patagonia Post Office). Turn left (east) on FR 58 and travel 3 miles to the trailhead on the southwest side of the road.

CREST TRAIL #103 SEGMENT OF ARIZONA TRAIL (MILLER PEAK TRAIL #105, BEND SPRING TRAIL #113, PAT SCOTT TRAIL #114, RAMSEY PEAK TRAIL #118)

Highlights: A trail to the high peaks of the Huachuca Mountains. Top-of-the-mountain views.

Total Distance: 11 miles. Your ride can be lengthened via connecting trails.

Location: Miller Peak Wilderness

Type of Trail: Equestrian/Hiker

Connecting Trails: Arizona Trail, Carr Peak Trail #107, Hamburg
 Trail #122, Comfort Springs Trail #109, Oversite Canyon Trail
 #112, Ida Canyon Trail #110, Sunnyside Canyon Trail #117
Difficulty: Difficult
Elevation: 6,550 to 9,050 feet
Best Months: Spring through fall
Maps: Coronado National Forest USGS: Montezuma Pass, Miller Peak
Special Considerations: No water is available.
Trailhead: From Sierra Vista, drive south on AZ 92 13 miles to the
 Coronado National Memorial Road (FR 61). Turn right (south)
 and continue 8.2 miles through the National Memorial to the top
 of Montezuma Pass. The trailhead is across the road from the
 parking lot.

SCOTIA CANYON TRAIL #127

Highlights: This is a segment Arizona Trail.
Total Distance: 6 miles. Your ride can be lengthened via connecting
 trails.
Location: Huachuca Mountains
Type of Trail: Equestrian/Hiker/Mountain Biker
Connecting Trails: Lakeshore Trail #128 at Parker Canyon Lake
Difficulty: Difficult
Elevation: 5,375 to 5,950 feet
Best Months: Year-round
Maps: Coronado National Forest USGS: Miller Peak
Special Considerations: Mountain bikers use this trail.
Trailhead: From Sierra Vista, drive south on AZ 92 13 miles to the
 junction of the Coronado National Memorial Road (FR 61). Turn
 right (south) and continue through the national memorial to Monte-
 zuma Pass. From the pass, continue on FR 61 about 8.4 miles to
 FR 48. Drive northwest on FR 48 for 3.1 miles to FR 228. Turn
 north on FR 228 and drive 2.5 miles to FR 204. Turn right on
 FR 204, which ends at the trailhead. This trail can also be accessed
 at Parker Canyon Lake and from Lakeside Trail #128.

SUNNYSIDE CANYON TRAIL #117

Highlights: Wildlife is abundant along this segment of the Arizona
  Trail. Use this trail for access to the Huachuca Crest.

Total Distance: 4.6 miles. Your ride can be lengthened via multiple
  connecting trails.

Location: Miller Peak Wilderness, Huachuca Mountains

Type of Trail: Equestrian/Hiker

Connecting Trails: Crest Trail #103, Eureka Mine Trail #129, Wake-
  field Trail #130

Difficulty: Difficult

Elevation: 5,950 to 8,475 feet

Best Months: Year-round

Maps: Coronado National Forest USGS: Huachuca Peak, Miller
  Peak

Special Considerations: There are multiple trail connections for
  travel into remote backcountry.

Trailhead: From Sierra Vista, drive south on AZ 92 13 miles to the
  Coronado Memorial Road (FR 61). Turn right and travel south
  through the national memorial to Montezuma Pass. From the pass,
  continue on FR 61 about 8.4 miles to FR 48. Drive northwest on
  FR 48 3.1 miles to FR 228. Go north on FR 228 about 2.5 miles
  to FR 204. Turn right on FR 204 and drive about 0.9 mile to the
  trailhead.

Safford Ranger District

Grant Goudy Ridge Trail #310

Highlights: A pleasant ride.

Total Distance: 8 miles. Your ride can be lengthened via connecting trails.

Location: Pinaleno Mountains

Type of Trail: Equestrian/Hiker

Connecting Trails: Grant Creek Trail #305

Difficulty: Difficult

Elevation: 9,500 to 5,000 feet

Best Months: Spring through fall

Maps: Coronado National Forest USGS: Webb Peak

Special Considerations: There is no water on the trail.

Trailhead: This trail has two access points. The first, at Soldier Creek Campground on the Swift Trail, is 9,500 feet in elevation. From Safford, travel south on US 191 to AZ 366. Turn right (southwest) and travel south and west 29 miles to the Soldier Creek Campground. The trailhead is at the rear of the campground on the left side of the road. (The campground is past the Columbine Information Center.) For the second, lower-elevation access, from Wilcox, drive north on US 191 to AZ 266. Turn left and go about 10 miles to FR 157. Or from Safford, travel south on US 191 past AZ 366, and continue 10 miles farther to AZ 266. Turn right and proceed to FR 157. Turn right on FR 157 to reach the trailhead. You will need to get a key from the Ft. Grant Administration Building for the locked gate on FR 157. Fort Grant is a state prison, and the trail meanders behind it. Four-wheel-drive may be required and you may want to park near the first creek crossing and ride to the trailhead. This trail begins at the junction with Grant Creek Trail #305.

Grant Creek Trail #305

Highlights: Great panoramic views. Cool streamside travel. Trout fishing. At the lower end of the trail, the trail ending is at historic Ft. Grant, which now serves as a state prison work camp.

Total Distance: 5.5 miles. Your ride can be lengthened via connecting trails.

Location: Pinaleno Mountains

Type of Trail: Equestrian/Hiker

Connecting Trails: Grant Goudy Ridge Trail #310

Difficulty: Difficult

Elevation: 5,200 to 8,895 feet

Best Months: Spring through fall

Maps: Coronado National Forest USGS: Webb Peak

Special Considerations: AZ 366 is closed November 15 through April 15, perhaps earlier depending on snowfall.

Trailhead: There are two access points. For the upper trailhead, from Safford, drive south on US 191 8 miles to the Swift Trail (AZ 366). Turn right (southwest) and travel 26 miles to the Cunningham Camp and the corral on the left side of the road. The trailhead is toward the back of the campground. For the lower trailhead, from Safford, drive south on US 191 17 miles to AZ 266. Turn right (southwest) and drive 19 miles to Bonita. Continue on AZ 266 to FR 157. Turn northeast. Stop at the Ft. Grant Administration Building for a key to the locked gate. Four-wheel-drive may be required, and you may want to park near the first creek crossing and ride to the trailhead. This trail begins at the junction with Grant Goudy Ridge Trail #310.

Dutch Henry Canyon Trail #297

Highlights: Desert-to-mountain trail. Occasional ladybug clustering.

Total Distance: 7.2 miles. Your ride can be lengthened via connecting trails.

Location: Pinaleno Mountains

Type of Trail: Equestrian/Hiker

Connecting Trails: Bear Canyon Trail #299

Difficulty: Difficult

Elevation: 3,838 to 8,120 feet

Best Months: Spring through fall

Maps: Coronado National Forest USGS: Stockton Pass

Special Considerations: No water is available.

Trailhead: Two trailheads access this trail. For the higher-elevation trail, from Safford, drive south on US 191 8 miles to AZ 366 (Swift Trail). Turn right (southwest) and drive 17 miles south to the Lady-bug Saddle. The trailhead to Bear Canyon Trail #299 is at the parking lot on the left side of the road. Take the Bear Canyon Trail 1.5 miles to reach the Dutch Henry Canyon Trail. For the lower elevation trailhead, from Safford, travel south on US 191 13 miles to FR 119. Turn right (west) and drive about 5 miles to the trailhead, which is near the windmill.

NUTTALL TRAIL #303

Highlights: A lengthy side trail that originates on the eastern aspect of Clark Peak Trail #301. This trail goes through some beautiful country, and can be a loop trail with any of the connecting trails.

Total Distance: 12.5 miles. Your ride can be lengthened via connecting trails.

Location: Mt. Graham Wilderness

Type of Trail: Equestrian/Hiker

Connecting Trails: Clark Peak Trail #301, Carter Nuttall Trail #315, Hells Hole Trail #319, Left Hand Canyon Trail #304A, Shingle Mill Loop Trail #35A

Difficulty: Difficult

Elevation: 5,400 to 8,440 feet

Best Months: Spring through fall

Maps: Coronado National Forest USGS: Blue Jay Peak, Webb Peak

Special Considerations: The Swift Trail (AZ 366 and FR 803) is closed November 15 through April 15. Snowstorms may extend the closing of the road.

Trailhead: From Safford, drive south on US 191 8 miles to the Swift Trail (AZ 366). Turn right (southwest) and drive 29 miles to the Columbine Visitor Information Station. Continue along FR 803 (Swift Trail) about 5 miles to the Riggs turnoff at the end of FR 803. The last 12 miles of this road to the trailhead are narrow and winding.

SYCAMORE TRAIL #278

Highlights: Remote and secluded. Wildlife is plentiful. Multiple connecting trails.

Total Distance: 5.5 miles. Your ride can be lengthened via connecting trails.

Location: Galiuro Wilderness

Type of Trail: Equestrian/Hiker

Connecting Trails: East Divide Trail #287, Powers Garden Trail #96, Tortilla Trail #254, Corral Canyon Trail #291

Difficulty: Very Difficult

Elevation: 4,800 to 6,000 feet

Best Months: Year-round

Maps: Coronado National Forest USGS: Kennedy Peak

Special Considerations: No water is available.

Trailhead: From Safford, drive south on US 191 17 miles to AZ 266. Turn right (southwest) and drive 19 miles to Bonita. From Bonita, drive north on the Aravaipa Road about 19 miles to the Deer Creek Ranch Road (FR 253). Turn left here and travel 8.4 miles to the trailhead for East Divide Trail #287. Ride and follow the East Divide Trail about 1 mile to the Mud Spring turnoff. Then follow the Mud Spring Trail 1 mile to the beginning of the Sycamore Trail.

EAST DIVIDE TRAIL #287

Highlights: Ridgetop trail with great views. Side trail, 0.25 mile to the top of Mt. Kennedy, or use the Bassett Peak Trail to the top of Mt. Bassett (7,663 feet).

Total Distance: 22.2 miles. Your ride can be lengthened via connecting trails.

Location: Galiuro Wilderness

Type of Trail: Equestrian/Hiker

Connecting Trails: High Creek Trail #290, Bassett Peak Trail #287, Tortilla Trail #254, Corral Canyon Trail #291, Paddy's River Trail #293, Sycamore Canyon Trail #278

Difficulty: Difficult

Elevation: 1,900 to 7,200 feet

Best Months: Year-round
Maps: Coronado National Forest USGS: Kennedy Peak, Bassett Peak
Special Considerations: Portions of this trail may be hard to find and
   follow. You may wish to take a map and compass with you.
Trailhead: From Safford, drive south on US 191 17 miles to AZ 266.
   Turn right (southwest) and drive 19 miles to Bonita. The northern,
   middle, and southern trailheads are accessible from Bonita. For the
   northern trailhead, from Bonita, drive north on the Aravaipa Road
   about 19 miles to the Deer Creek Ranch Road (FR 253). Turn left
   and drive 8.4 miles to the East Divide trailhead. The Tortilla Trail is
   accessible from this point as well. For the southern trailhead, from
   Bonita, drive west on the Aravaipa Road 13 miles to FR 651. Turn
   left (south) and drive 3.5 miles to FR 660, a four-wheel-drive road.
   Turn right and travel 2 miles to the East Divide trailhead. For the
   middle trailhead, from Bonita, go west on Sunset Road (which becomes FR 651) and drive 13 miles to FR 159. Turn west on FR 159
   and go 4 miles to the trailhead. The trail starts 1.5 miles down High
   Creek Trail #290. There is a 2,000-foot elevation change in this
   1.5-mile route. This access is very steep and recommended only
   for experienced riders with experienced trail horses.

POWERS GARDEN TRAIL #96

Highlights: Extremely remote wilderness with great scenery. His-
   toric setting and multiple trail connections.
Total Distance: 8.9 miles. Your ride can be lengthened via connecting
   trails.
Location: Galiuro Wilderness
Type of Trail: Equestrian/Hiker
Connecting Trails: West Divide Trail #289, Southfield Trail #296,
   Pipestem Trail #271 at 4.4 miles, Tent Lookout Trail #294, Corral
   Canyon Trail #291 (to Kennedy Peak), Tortilla Trail #254,
   Sycamore Canyon Trail #278
Difficulty: Difficult
Elevation: 4,660 to 5,280 feet
Best Months: Year-round

Maps: Coronado National Forest USGS: Kennedy Park

Special Considerations: This trail can be hard to follow in areas; use a topo map and compass. The old Powers Cabin is located on West Divide Trail #289.

Trailhead: From Safford, drive west on US 70 13.5 miles. Turn left (west) onto the Klondyke Road, and continue 32 miles to the Aravaipa Road. Turn left and travel northwest for 3.5 miles to the old Powers Garden Road (FR 96). Turn south and drive 11 miles to the trailhead. FR 96 is listed as a four-wheel-drive road. Access is available at Deer Creek and High Creek.

TAYLOR CANYON TRAIL #306

Highlights: Access to the high country.

Total Distance: 5.7 miles. Your ride can be lengthened via connecting trails.

Location: Pinaleno Mountains

Type of Trail: Equestrian/Hiker

Connecting Trails: Clark Peak Trail #301

Difficulty: Difficult

Elevation: 4,800 to 7,150 feet

Best Months: Spring through fall

Maps: Coronado National Forest USGS: Blue Jay Peak

Special Considerations: Water is usually available at Colter Spring.

Trailhead: There are two access points. For the northern trailhead, from Safford, drive west on US 70 through Pima to the Tripp Canyon Road (FR 286). Turn left (west) and follow this road to the Taylor Canyon sign. Turn left (south) and follow FR 156 6 miles to the North Taylor Canyon trailhead. For the southern trailhead, from Safford, drive south on US 191 17 miles to AZ 266. Turn right (southwest) and drive 19 miles to Bonita. From Bonita, drive north on the Aravaipa Road about 2.5 miles to FR 509. Turn north on this four-wheel-drive road. Drive past the Seventy-Six Ranch House on the east, and continue about 5 miles to the national forest boundary. Park here and ride the last stretch to the trailhead.

CORRAL CANYON TRAIL #291

Highlights: Remote wilderness. Great views. Multiple connecting trails.

Total Distance: 4.2 miles. Your ride can be lengthened via connecting trails.

Location: Galiuro Wilderness

Type of Trail: Equestrian/Hiker

Connecting Trails: Powers Garden Trail #96, East Divide Trail #287, Tortilla Trail #254

Difficulty: Difficult

Elevation: 4,800 to 6,800 feet

Best Months: Year-round

Maps: Coronado National Forest, Galiuro Wilderness USGS: Kennedy Peak

Special Considerations: Water is generally available at Corral Spring and Powers Garden. This trail is easy to follow, but a map and a compass in the remote backcountry would be helpful.

Trailhead: From Safford, drive south on US 191 17 miles to AZ 266. Turn right (southwest) and drive 19 miles to Bonita. From Bonita, continue north on the Aravaipa Road about 19 miles to the Deer Creek Ranch Road (FR 253). Turn left and drive 8.4 miles to the trailhead for Tortilla Trail #254 and East Divide Trail #287. The latter will bring you to the Corral Canyon Trail in 5 miles. Or, to access from the Powers Garden Trail, from Safford, drive west on US 70 13.5 miles. Turn left (west) onto the Klondyke Road, and continue 32 miles to the Aravaipa Road. Turn right and travel northwest 3.5 miles to the old Powers Garden Road (FR 96). Turn south and drive 11 miles to the trailhead. FR 96 is listed as a four-wheel-drive road. Access is available at Deer Creek and High Creek.

SHAKE TRAIL #309

Highlights: Great views of the Greasewood Mountains and the Sulphur Springs valley. Easy access.

Total Distance: 4.8 miles

Location: Pinaleno Mountains

Type of Trail: Equestrian/Hiker
Difficulty: Difficult
Elevation: 8,500 to 5,500 feet
Best Months: Spring through fall
Maps: Coronado National Forest
Special Considerations: This trail is quite steep. Water is available only at Stockton Pass.
Trailhead: There are two access points. For the northern access, from Safford, travel south on US 191 8 miles to AZ 366. Turn right (southwest) and follow this road (Swift Trail) 17.5 miles to the trailhead. The southern access point is at Stockton Pass Picnic Area. From Safford, travel south on US 191 17 miles to AZ 266. Turn right (southwest) on AZ 266, which becomes FR 198, and drive about 12 miles to the Stockton Pass Picnic Area and the trailhead.

TORTILLA TRAIL #254

Highlights: A remote trail in open wilderness. In spots this trail may be difficult to follow because it intersects with ranch cattle trails.
Total Distance: 8.2 miles. Your ride can be lengthened via connecting trails.
Location: Galiuro Wilderness
Type of Trail: Equestrian/Hiker
Connecting Trails: Powers Garden Trail #96, Sycamore Canyon Trail #278, Salt Trap Trail #256, East Divide Trail #287
Difficulty: Difficult
Elevation: 5,000 to 6,000 feet
Best Months: Year-round
Maps: Coronado National Forest USGS: Kennedy Peak
Special Considerations: Generally, water may be found at Mud Spring and Powers Garden Spring.
Trailhead: From Safford, drive south on US 191 17 miles to AZ 266. Turn right (southwest) and drive 19 miles to Bonita. Continue north from Bonita on the Aravaipa Road 19 miles to the Deer Creek Ranch Road (FR 253). Turn left and drive 8.4 miles to the trailhead.

SHINGLE MILL MESA TRAIL #35

Highlights: An old Jeep trail.

Total Distance: 6.1 miles. Your ride can be lengthened via connecting trails.

Location: Pinaleno Mountains

Type of Trail: Equestrian/Hiker

Connecting Trails: Ash Creek Trail #307

Difficulty: Moderate

Elevation: 5,000 to 7,800 feet

Best Months: Spring through fall

Maps: Coronado National Forest USGS: Webb Peak

Special Considerations: No water is available.

Trailhead: From Pima, travel south on the Cottonwood Washington Road to FR 681. Turn right on FR 681 and continue about 4 miles. You will reach a gate; proceed through the gate and at 0.2 mile, the trail begins on the right. Or, access this trail from the Columbine Public Corrals and Ash Creek Trail #35.

LADYBUG TRAIL #329

Highlights: This trail leads Bear Canyon Trail #299, crossing Jacobsen Ridge and ending in a commercial fruit orchard.

Total Distance: 5.9 miles. Your ride can be lengthened via connecting trails.

Location: Pinaleno Mountains

Type of Trail: Equestrian/Hiker

Connecting Trails: Bear Canyon Trail #299

Difficulty: Difficult

Elevation: 8,500 to 5,100 feet

Best Months: Spring through fall

Maps: Coronado National Forest USGS: Webb Peak

Special Considerations: Travel downhill from the upper trailhead is quite steep.

Trailhead: From Safford, travel south on US 191 about 8 miles to AZ 366 (Swift Trail). Turn right (southwest) and travel 17 miles. The trailhead is located at Ladybug. There is a saddle adjacent to

AZ 366. During the winter, with the closure of US 191, you can access Bear Canyon Trail #299 from AZ 266. Follow the Bear Canyon Trail to the Ladybug Trail. Do not use the upper trailhead for winter access as it may be snowed in.

BEAR CANYON TRAIL #299

Highlights: A south-facing trail. On occasion, clustering ladybugs.
Total Distance: 6 miles. Your ride can be lengthened via connecting trails.
Location: Pinaleno Mountains
Type of Trail: Equestrian/Hiker
Connecting Trails: Dutch Henry Trail #297, Ladybug Trail #329, Shingle Mill Mesa Trail #35
Difficulty: Moderate
Elevation: 4,920 to 8,720 feet
Best Months: Spring through fall
Maps: Coronado National Forest USGS: Stockton Pass, Ft. Grant, Mt. Graham
Special Considerations: AZ 366 is closed to traffic from November 1 through April 15.
Trailhead: From Safford, travel south on US 191 about 8 miles to AZ 366 (Swift Trail). Turn right (southwest) and travel 17 miles. The trailhead is located at Ladybug. There is a saddle adjacent to AZ 366. During the winter, with the closure of US 191, from Bonita, travel east on AZ 266 12–14 miles to Bear Canyon Trail #299.

WEBB PEAK TRAIL #345

Highlights: A connecting spur trail to the Webb Peak Lookout.
Total Distance: 2.8 miles. Your ride can be lengthened via connecting trails.
Location: Pinaleno Mountains
Type of Trail: Equestrian/Hiker
Connecting Trails: Ash Creek Trail #307
Difficulty: Difficult
Elevation: 9,120 to 9,960 feet

Best Months: Spring through fall
Maps: Coronado National Forest USGS: Webb Peak
Trailhead: From Safford, drive south on US 191 8 miles to AZ 366
(Swift Trail). Turn right (southwest) and drive 29 miles to the
Columbine Vista Information Station. Just past the station on
your right are public horse corrals. Parking is available. Or, you
may continue along the Swift Trail to the Webb Peak Road. Turn
off to the park.

DEAD MAN TRAIL #70

Highlights: Year-round stream and waterfalls.
Total Distance: 3.4 miles. Your ride can be lengthened via connecting
trails.
Location: Pinaleno Mountains
Type of Trail: Equestrian/Hiker
Connecting Trails: Round the Mountain Trail #302
Difficulty: Difficult
Elevation: 4,560 to 6,280 feet
Best Months: Spring through fall
Maps: Coronado National Forest USGS: Mt. Graham
Special Considerations: Four-wheel-drive vehicles are needed to
access the trailhead.
Trailhead: From Safford, drive northwest on US 70. Turn south on
20th Avenue. Turn right (west) on Golf Course Road. In about
0.5 mile, at the intersection, bear left 45 degrees. Follow this road
to the Pipeline Road (not marked). To reach the trailhead, you
will need to weave in and around and behind the Thatcher
Campground. The road is rough and narrow and passes through
several gates.

FRYE CANYON TRAIL #36

Highlights: Access to Round the Mountain Trail.
Total Distance: 2.8 miles. Your ride can be lengthened via connecting
trails.
Location: Pinaleno Mountains

Type of Trail: Equestrian/Hiker
Connecting Trails: Round the Mountain Trail #302, Ash Ridge Trail
  #327
Difficulty: Easy
Elevation: 5,350 to 7,120 feet
Best Months: Year-round
Maps: Coronado National Forest USGS: Mt. Graham
Special Considerations: There is usually water in Frye Creek.
Trailhead: From Safford, drive northwest on US 70 to Thatcher. Turn
  left (south) on Stadium Street and follow it to FR 103. The trail-
  head is at the end of this road, 10 miles beyond the Frye Mesa
  Reservoir. The last miles of FR 103 are rough and rocky.

ROUND THE MOUNTAIN TRAIL #302

Highlights: A beautiful but rugged trail. Excellent horse trail. Horse
  corral at lower-elevation trailhead.
Total Distance: 14.3 miles. Your ride can be lengthened via connect-
  ing trails.
Location: Pinaleno Mountains
Type of Trail: Equestrian/Hiker
Connecting Trails: Noon Creek Ridge Trail #318, Gibson Canyon
  Trail #308, Frye Canyon Trail #36
Difficulty: Difficult
Elevation: 5,600 to 9,600 feet
Best Months: Spring through fall
Maps: Coronado National Forest USGS: Mt. Graham, Webb Peak
Trailhead: There are two access points. For the Swift Trail, from
  Safford, travel south on US 191 about 18 miles to AZ 366. Turn
  right and travel southwest about 8 miles to the Round the Mountain
  trailhead and picnic area on the right side of the road. This trailhead
  provides access to the east open aspect of the trail. To reach the west-
  ern portion of this trail, continue on 21 miles past the first Round the
  Mountain trailhead to the Columbine Visitor Information Station.
  Turn right on FR 508 toward the summer home area. Park on the
  roadside and ride 1 mile to the trailhead. Do not block the gate.

ARCADIA TRAIL #328

Highlights: Part of the national recreation trail between the Arcadia and Shannon Campgrounds.

Total Distance: 5.1 miles. Your ride can be lengthened via connecting trails.

Location: Pinaleno Mountains

Type of Trail: Equestrian/Hiker

Connecting Trails: Heliograph Trail #328A, Noon Creek Ridge Trail #318

Difficulty: Difficult

Elevation: 9,100 to 6,100 feet

Best Months: Spring through fall

Maps: Coronado National Forest USGS: Mt. Graham

Special Considerations: No water is available. Camping areas are located along the trail.

Trailhead: From Safford, travel south on US 191 about 10 miles to AZ 366 (Swift Trail). Turn right and travel southwest. Follow the signs to the trailhead and campground.

WEST DIVIDE TRAIL #289

Highlights: Top-of-the-mountain panoramic views, with multiple side trails. This trail ends at Maverick Peak.

Total Distance: 23.7 miles. Your ride can be lengthened via connecting trails.

Location: Galiuro Wilderness

Type of Trail: Equestrian/Hiker

Connecting Trails: Southfield Trail #296, Tent Lookout Trail #294, Pipestem Trail #271, Yle Trail #288, Powers Garden Trail #96

Difficulty: Difficult

Elevation: 4,260 to 6,800 feet

Best Months: Year-round

Maps: Coronado National Forest USGS: Bassett Park, Kennedy Peak

Special Considerations: The trail may be hard to find in areas, so bring a map and a compass.

Trailhead: From the Muleshoe Ranch (Hookers Hot Springs on forest service map), take FR 691 north 13.5 miles, just prior to the Jackson cabin. This route will require four-wheel-drive. Or, access this trail from Powers Garden Trail #96. From Safford, drive west on US 70 13.5 miles. Turn left (west) onto the Klondyke Road, and continue 32 miles to the Aravaipa Road. Turn right and travel northwest 3.5 miles to the old Powers Garden Road (FR 96). Turn south and drive 11 miles to the trailhead. FR 96 is listed as a four-wheel-drive road. Access is available at Deer Creek and High Creek.

HELIOGRAPH TRAIL #328A

Highlights: A connecting spur trail from the Arcadia Trail #328 to Heliograph Peak.
Total Distance: 1 mile. Your ride can be lengthened via connecting trails.
Location: Pinaleno Mountains
Type of Trail: Equestrian/Hiker
Connecting Trails: Arcadia Trail #328
Difficulty: Difficult
Elevation: 9,200 to 10,022 feet
Best Months: Spring through fall
Maps: Coronado National Forest USGS: Mt. Graham
Special Considerations: Be sure to read the interpretive sign at the Heliograph Lookout so you can better understand and appreciate the history that surrounds you.
Trailhead: From Safford, travel south on US 191 8 miles to the Swift Trail (AZ 366). Turn right (southwest) and drive 22 miles to the entrance of the Shannon Campground and the road to the Heliograph Peak Lookout. At the rear of Shannon Campground, take Arcadia Trail #328 1 mile to access Heliograph Trail #328A. (See page 103 for Arcadia Trail #328.)

BLUE JAY RIDGE TRAIL #314

Highlights: A connecting trail with loop potential. Great views.
Total Distance: 3.2 miles. Your ride can be lengthened via connecting trails.

Location: Pinaleno Mountains
Type of Trail: Equestrian/Hiker
Connecting Trails: Clark Peak Trail #301
Difficulty: Difficult
Elevation: 7,400 to 8,680 feet
Best Months: Spring through fall
Maps: Coronado National Forest USGS: Blue Jay Peak
Trailhead: There are two access points. From Safford, drive northwest on US 70 through Pima to the Tripp Canyon Road (FR 286), past the Taylor Canyon turnoff. Turn left and continue 16.4 miles to a bend in the road at Turkey Spring. The trailhead is here. Or, continue on FR 286 an additional 1.5 miles. Prior to the gate for the tower is a trailhead to Clark Peak Trail #301. Follow trail #301 (old roadbed) about 1 mile to where the trail forks to the east. Follow this old road for an additional 0.5 mile to Blue Jay Ridge Trail #314.

ASH CREEK TRAIL #307 AND ASH CREEK DETOUR TRAIL #307A

Highlights: A pleasant trail that leads from the public corrals at Columbine to Cluff Ponds south of Pima. Remains of an old logging operation can be found. Trout fishing in Ash Creek.
Total Distance: 8.2 miles. Equine detour #307A 0.9 mile.
Location: Pinaleno Mountains
Type of Trail: Equestrian/Hiker
Difficulty: Difficult
Elevation: 9,500 to 4,200 feet
Best Months: Spring through fall
Maps: Coronado National Forest USGS: Webb Peak
Special Considerations: AZ 366 is closed November 15 through April 15. There are camping areas along the trail. A stretch of this trail contains slickrock, which can be hazardous to horses; use Trail #307A to bypass this area.
Trailhead: From Safford, travel south on US 191 about 8 miles to AZ 366 (Swift Trail). Turn right and travel southwest about 29 miles. Follow the signs to the Columbine work area. You will come upon Webb Peak Road ("Road Closed to Motorized Vehicles"). Park

here and ride up the road to the tower. East of the tower is a trail to the Columbine Public Corrals. At about 400–500 feet is an unnamed trail to the left, which leads to Ash Creek Trail #307. This trail loops back to the corrals. Regardless of your starting point, at the Webb Peak Road or Columbine Corrals, you will need to proceed down FR 803 about 0.1 mile. To access the lower-elevation trailhead, from Pima, travel south on Cluff Ranch Road. When you reach the entrance, turn left. Cross the cattle guard and continue on until you reach a three-way intersection. Turn left and follow the road 1 mile to the trailhead.

Santa Catalina Ranger District

TURKEY CREEK TRAIL #34

Highlights: The landscape is consistent with the Sonoran Desert. Part of the Arizona Trail, this trail also provides access to the Saguaro National Monument.

Total Distance: 6 miles

Location: Rincon Mountain Wilderness

Type of Trail: Equestrian/Hiker

Difficulty: Difficult

Elevation: 4,600 to 6,600 feet

Best Months: Fall through Spring

Maps: Coronado National Forest USGS: Happy Valley

Special Considerations: Water is generally found along the trail, except in the hottest and driest periods.

Trailhead: From Tucson, drive east on I-10 39 miles to the J-Six-Mescal Road (exit 297). Turn north on Mescal Road and drive 16.4 miles to FR 4408. Turn left and travel 0.4 mile. Pass through the gate to the parking lot with the large sycamore trees. The trail starts on the opposite side of the creek and follows the road for 1.5 miles.

ASPEN LOOP TRAIL #93

Highlights: A loop trail when used to connect other trails in Pusch Ridge Wilderness, which can provide a lengthy ride through beautiful country.

Total Distance: 3.8 miles. Your ride can be lengthened via connecting trails.

Location: Pusch Ridge Wilderness

Type of Trail: Equestrian/Hiker

Connecting Trails: Marshall Gulch Trail #3, Wilderness of Rock Trail #44

Difficulty: Difficult

Elevation: 7,410 to 8,400 feet

Best Months: Year-round.

Maps: Coronado National Forest USGS: Mt. Lemmon

Special Considerations: There may be heavy snowfields during the winter.

Trailhead: From Tucson, take the Tanque Verde Road east and north to the Catalina Highway. Turn left and drive 4.2 miles to the forest boundary. Continue 26 miles through Summerhaven to the Marshall Gulch picnic area.

MARSHALL GULCH TRAIL #3

Highlights: This connecting trail offers a cool, shady ride with a rich view and many wildflowers.

Total Distance: 1.3 miles. Your ride can be lengthened via connecting trails.

Location: Pusch Ridge Wilderness

Type of Trail: Equestrian/Hiker

Connecting Trails: Aspen Loop Trail #93, Wilderness of Rock Trail #44

Difficulty: Difficult

Elevation: 7,410 to 8,400 feet

Best Months: Year-round

Maps: Coronado National Forest USGS: Mt. Lemmon

Special Considerations: There may be heavy snowfields during the winter.

Trailhead: From Tucson, take the Tanque Verde Road east and north to the Catalina Highway. Turn left and drive 4.2 miles to the forest boundary. Continue 26 miles through Summerhaven to the Marshall Gulch picnic area.

WILDERNESS OF ROCK TRAIL #44

Highlights: This trail contains outstanding rock formations with a diversity of climatic settings. Natural rock garden.

Total Distance: 4 miles. Your ride can be lengthened via connecting trails.

Location: Pusch Ridge Wilderness

Type of Trail: Equestrian/Hiker

Connecting Trails: Marshall Gulch Trail #3, Mt. Lemmon Trail #5,
Romero Trail #8, Aspen Loop Trail #93, West Fork Trail #24
Difficulty: Difficult
Elevation: 7,000 to 8,000 feet
Best Months: Year-round
Maps: Coronado National Forest USGS: Mt. Lemmon
Special Considerations: There is usually water for horses in Lemmon
Creek. There may be snowfields in the winter.
Trailhead: There are many access points, but all are from other trails.
You would probably best be served by using the access to Marshall
Gulch Trail #3. From Tucson, take the Tanque Verde Road east and
north to the Catalina Highway. Turn left and drive 4.2 miles to the
forest boundary. Continue 26 miles through Summerhaven to the
Marshall Gulch picnic area.

MT. LEMMON TRAIL #5

Highlights: Access to the Wilderness of Rock area. Expansive views.
This trail is a segment of the Arizona Trail.
Total Distance: 5.8 miles. Your ride can be lengthened via connecting
trails.
Location: Pusch Ridge Wilderness.
Type of Trail: Equestrian/Hiker.
Connecting Trails: Wilderness of Rock Trail #44, West Fork Trail
#24, Sutherland Trail #6, Lemmon Rock Lookout Trail #12,
Romero Trail #8.
Difficulty: Difficult.
Elevation: 7,500 to 9,100 feet
Best Months: Year-round. Snow may close the trail in the winter.
Maps: Coronado National Forest USGS: Mt. Lemmon.
Special Considerations: The section of this trail between the Wilder-
ness of Rock Trail #44 and the West Fork Trail #24 is very steep
and should be attempted only by experienced riders with experi-
enced horses.
Trailhead: From Tucson, take the Tanque Verde Road east and north
to the Catalina Highway. Turn left and drive 4.2 miles to the forest

boundary. Continue 28 miles past the Mt. Lemmon Ski Area to the power substation on Radio Ridge. Ride west on the trail to a dirt road. The trail junction is farther down the dirt road.

CAÑADA DEL ORO TRAIL #4

Highlights: "Canyon of Gold." Old mines and shacks. Big canyon. Visit Catalina Camp.

Total Distance: 7.7 miles. Your ride can be lengthened via connecting trails.

Location: Santa Catalina Mountains

Type of Trail: Equestrian/Hiker

Connecting Trails: Red Ridge Trail #2

Difficulty: Difficult

Elevation: 4,800 to 7,600 feet

Best Months: Year-round

Maps: Coronado National Forest USGS: Oracle

Special Considerations: Winter snows may close the access from the Steward Observatory.

Trailhead: There are two ways to access this trail, one from atop Mt. Lemmon at the Stewart Observatory and the other from a lower elevation using Charoleau Gap Road. For the observatory, from Tucson, take the Tanque Verde Road east and north to the Catalina Highway. Turn left and follow the highway to the top. Just prior to the Steward Observatory is a parking lot. Park here. Ride down Mt. Lemmon Trail #5 and Sutherland Trail #6 to the Cañada del Oro Trail #4. For the Charoleau Gap Road (four-wheel-drive), drive north from Tucson on AZ 89 (Oracle Road) about 23 miles to Golden Ranch Road. Turn east and drive about 1 mile. Turn north on Largo del Oro Road. Travel approximately 2 miles to a dirt road (FR 736), as this road turns east along the riverbed. Follow this road left at a "Private Property" sign, through the riverbed and up over Samonrigo Ridge to the trailhead.

WEST FORK TRAIL #24

Highlights: A segment of the Arizona Trail, this streamside trail offers prospects of seeing abundant wildlife.

Total Distance: 6.8 miles. Your ride can be lengthened via connecting trails.

Location: Pusch Ridge Wilderness

Type of Trail: Equestrian/Hiker

Connecting Trails: Sabino Canyon Trail #23, Bear Canyon Trail #29, Romero Trail #8, Mt. Lemmon Trail #5, Box Camp Trail #22

Difficulty: Difficult

Elevation: 4,300 to 6,100 feet

Best Months: Year-round

Maps: Coronado National Forest USGS: Mt. Lemmon

Special Considerations: Treat the riparian areas through which the trail travels with care. There are several creek crossings, which are difficult with high water.

Trailhead: This trail must be accessed from other trails. Access to the West Fork Trail is 2.5 miles from the Sabino Canyon trailhead. On Bear Canyon Trail #29, it begins at 10.3 miles. The connection on Romero Trail #8 is at 5.6 miles. On Mt. Lemmon Trail #5, it is at 5.8 miles. On Box Camp Trail #22, it is at 7.1 miles.

SABINO CANYON TRAIL #23

Highlights: This connecting trail offers spectacular views.

Total Distance: 2.5 miles. Your ride can be lengthened via connecting trails.

Location: Pusch Ridge Wilderness

Type of Trail: Equestrian/Hiker

Connecting Trails: East Fork Trail #24A, Bear Canyon Trail #29, Phone Line Trail #27

Difficulty: Difficult

Elevation: 2,700 to 5,000 feet

Best Months: Fall through spring

Maps: Coronado National Forest USGS: Sabino Canyon

Special Considerations: If you choose to loop your ride, you will need to use Phone Line Trail #27.

Trailhead: From Tucson, take the Tanque Verde Road north to Sabino Canyon Visitor Center. Park here and take the designated horse trail along the Shuttle Bus Road to the trailhead.

ROMERO TRAIL #8

Highlights: Waterfalls and great views with access to Sabino Canyon.

Total Distance: 6.6 miles. Your ride can be lengthened via connecting trails.

Location: Pusch Ridge Wilderness

Type of Trail: Equestrian/Hiker

Connecting Trails: Sutherland Trail #6, Mt. Lemmon Trail #5, West Fork Trail #24

Difficulty: Difficult

Elevation: 2,800 to 6,000 feet

Best Months: Spring through fall

Maps: Coronado National Forest, Pusch Ridge Wilderness USGS: Oro Valley, Mt. Lemmon

Special Considerations: This is a rugged and difficult trail that should only be attempted by experienced riders and trail horses.

Trailhead: From Tucson, travel north on US 89 (Oracle Road) to Catalina State Park. The trailhead is within the park. There is a park entrance fee.

BOX CAMP TRAIL #22 AND
BOX SPRING TRAIL #22A

Highlights: Perhaps some of the best views in the Santa Catalina District, but the trail is steep and rocky. Interesting side trip to Box Spring via Box Spring Trail #22A (at 0.9 mile).

Total Distance: 7.1 miles. Your ride can be lengthened via connecting trails.

Location: Pusch Ridge Wilderness

Type of Trail: Equestrian/Hiker

Connecting Trails: Sabino Canyon Trail #23, East Fork Trail #24A

Difficulty: Difficult

Elevation: 3,700 to 8,050 feet

Best Months: Year-round

Maps: Coronado National Forest USGS: Mt. Lemmon, Sabino Canyon

Special Considerations: This trail is best done with experienced trail horses.

Trailhead: From Tucson, travel north on the Catalina Highway to the Spencer Canyon turnoff (MP 22). The trailhead is 100–150 yards uphill from the turnoff.

SUTHERLAND TRAIL #6

Highlights: A rugged trail following the power-line access along the ridge.
Total Distance: 8.7 miles. Your ride can be lengthened via connecting trails.
Location: Along the Pusch Ridge Wilderness
Type of Trail: Equestrian/Hiker
Connecting Trails: Mt. Lemmon Trail #5, Samaniego Ridge Trail #7, Cañada del Oro Trail #4
Difficulty: Difficult
Elevation: 2,700 to 8,600 feet
Best Months: Spring through fall
Maps: Coronado National Forest USGS: Oro Valley, Mt. Lemmon
Special Considerations: This trail is best done with experienced trail horses.
Trailhead: From Tucson, travel north on the Catalina Highway to the Spencer Canyon turnoff (MP 22). The trailhead is 100–150 yards uphill from the turnoff.

RED RIDGE TRAIL #2

Highlights: This trail leads to an old post named Catalina Camp. An ideal trail for connecting to Cañada del Oro Trail #4.
Total Distance: 5 miles. Your ride can be lengthened via connecting trails.
Location: Santa Catalina Mountains
Type of Trail: Equestrian/Hiker
Connecting Trails: Catalina Camp Trail #401, Cañada del Oro Trail #4, Mt. Lemmon Trail #5
Difficulty: Difficult
Elevation: 4,880 to 8,080 feet
Best Months: Spring through fall
Maps: Coronado National Forest USGS: Mt. Lemmon

Trailhead: From Tucson, take the Catalina Highway north from Tanque Verde Road. Drive past the forest boundary and continue about 32 miles to the trailhead on the north side of the road just before the ski area.

EAST FORK TRAIL #24A

Highlights: A connecting trail with spectacular views.
Total Distance: 2.6 miles. Your ride can be lengthened via connecting trails.
Location: Rusch Ridge Wilderness
Type of Trail: Equestrian/Hiker
Connecting Trails: Sabino Canyon Trail #23, Bear Canyon Trail #29, Phone Line Trail #27
Difficulty: Difficult
Elevation: 2,700 to 5,000 feet
Best Months: Fall through spring
Maps: Coronado National Forest USGS: Sabino Canyon
Special Considerations: If you choose to loop your ride, you will need to use Phone Line Trail #27.
Trailhead: From Tucson, take the Tanque Verde Road north to Sabino Canyon Visitor Center. Park here and take the designated horse trail along the shuttle bus road to the trailhead.

BEAR CANYON TRAIL #29

Highlights: Spectacular views.
Total Distance: 8.3 miles. Your ride can be lengthened via connecting trails.
Location: Pusch Ridge Wilderness
Type of Trail: Equestrian/Hiker
Connecting Trails: Phone Line Trail #27, East Fork Trail #24A
Difficulty: Difficult
Elevation: 2,700 to 5,000 feet
Best Months: Fall through spring
Maps: Coronado National Forest USGS: Sabino Canyon
Special Considerations: If you choose to loop your ride, you will need to use Phone Line Trail #27

Trailhead: From Tucson, take the Tanque Verde Road north to Sabino Canyon Visitor Center. Park here and take the designated horse trail along the shuttle bus road to the trailhead.

PALISADE TRAIL #99

Highlights: A fairly wooded trail with panoramic views.
Total Distance: 6.2 miles. Your ride can be lengthened via connecting trails.
Location: Pusch Ridge Wilderness
Type of Trail: Equestrian/Hiker
Connecting Trails: East Fork Trail #24A, Bear Canyon Trail #29, Sabino Canyon Trail #23
Difficulty: Difficult
Elevation: 4,100 to 7,800 feet
Best Months: Year-round
Maps: Coronado National Forest USGS: Mt. Bigelow, Sabino Canyon
Special Considerations: For experienced trail horses and experienced riders only. The trail may be hard to find, as it drops into lower Pine Canyon. Water is generally available at Mud Springs. Very hot in the summer and possible snowfields in the winter.
Trailhead: From Tucson, take the Catalina Highway north from the Tanque Verde Road. Drive 4.2 miles to the forest boundary, then continue 19 miles to the Organization Ridge Road, which is just past the Palisade Visitor Center and is closed in winter. Drive down the Organization Ridge Road 0.25 miles to the trailhead. When the Organization Ridge Road is closed to vehicles in the winter, you may still ride your horse to the trailhead.

BRUSH CORRAL TRAIL #19

Highlights: This trail leads to a historic forest ranger station that has not been used since World War I.
Total Distance: 7.4 miles. Your ride can be lengthened via connecting trails.
Location: Santa Catalina Mountains
Type of Trail: Equestrian/Hiker

Connecting Trails: Green Mountain Trail #21, Short Tail Trail #21A
Difficulty: Difficult
Elevation: 7,000 to 3,800 feet
Best Months: Fall through spring
Maps: Coronado National Forest USGS: Mt. Bigelow
Special Considerations: The trail may be difficult to find in areas, so bring a compass and a topographic map.
Trailhead: From Tucson, take the Catalina Highway north to the San Pedro Vista Point trailhead for Green Mt. Trail #21. Ride on Trail #21 for 0.3 mile to the Brush Corral Trail.

GREEN MOUNTAIN TRAIL #21

Highlights: Good vistas in forested (pine and fir) areas.
Total Distance: 3.6 miles. Your ride can be lengthened via connecting trails.
Location: Santa Catalina Mountains
Type of Trail: Equestrian/Hiker
Connecting Trails: Shortcut Trail #21A, Maverick Spring Trail #704, Brush Corral Trail #19
Difficulty: Difficult
Elevation: 6,000 to 7,300 feet
Best Months: Spring through fall
Maps: Coronado National Forest USGS: Mt. Bigelow
Special Considerations: Take a short side trip to Maverick Spring (0.4 mile). The spring usually has water and the surrounding area is quite lush.
Trailhead: From Tucson, drive north on the Catalina Highway either to the General Hitchcock Campground or San Pedro Vista Point Trailhead. Directions to both trailheads are clearly marked. If you use the General Hitchcock Campground trailhead, the trail is located behind the metal trailhead sign. There are many paths in this area; fortunately, they all converge at the trail.

Kaibab National Forest

THE KAIBAB is a 1.6 million–acre forest that, along with the Coronado National Forest, is an archeological gem. The Kaibab National Forest surrounds Grand Canyon National Park. It has two divisions: North Kaibab and South Kaibab. The South Kaibab is slightly longer, and is bordered on the south by the Prescott National Forest and on the east by the Coconino National Forest. The North Kaibab is a high plateau with pine and oak forests and is bordered by the Grand Canyon and the Utah border. The Kaibab is generally composed of ponderosa forests and has extremely rugged terrain. Elevations range from 5,500 feet to the 10,418-foot Mt. Kendrick.

Historically, the Kaibab area was the land of hunters and gatherers. Most of the archeological remains are 850 to 1,200 years old. The Cohonina were the first known people to live here, gradually giving way to the Anasasi and Hopi tribes. About 1350, the Havasupai and the Hualopai from the west, the Yavapai from the south, and the Navajo from the east began to settle in the Kaibab. The Spaniards visited the area in 1540, followed by Captain Lorenzo Sitgreaves's 1851 expedition. The escort for the Sitgreaves expedition was Major Kendrick, for whom Kendrick Mountain is named. Bill Williams Mountain is named after the infamous mountain man William Sheerly Williams. Lt. Edward Fitzgerald Beale brought an expedition by wagon in 1859–1860, and built the wagon trail that bears his name. In the mid- to late nineteenth century, the Spanish friars Dominguez and Escalante lived among and worked at Christianizing the native peoples. Joseph Hamblin, a Mormon, also explored and passed through the Kaibab area. The settlers tried to farm the open meadows of the Kaibab by digging irrigation wells and planting root vegetables, but their efforts were largely unsuccessful. Because of the dryness of the area, their wells were not able to support their farms.

Kaibab National Forest Trails

Williams Ranger District
Kaibab National Forest
Williams Ranger District
Route 1, Box 142
Williams, AZ 86046
928-635-2633

Nearby Cities
Williams, Parks, Perkinsville,
Ashfork

North Kaibab Ranger District
Kaibab National Forest
North Kaibab Ranger District
Box 248
Fredonia, AZ 86022
928-643-7395

Nearby City
Fredonia

Tusayan Ranger District
Kaibab National Forest
Tusayan Ranger District
PO Box 3088
Tusayan, AZ 86023
928-638-2443

Nearby City
Tusayan

Page   Trails
133   Arizona Trail (Coconino
         Rim via Russell Wash to
         Moqui Stage Station)

Williams Ranger District

BILL WILLIAMS MOUNTAIN TRAIL #21

Highlights: This trail was used as a toll road in 1902. The builder, Esau Lamb, charged a fee for riders and hikers to travel to the top of Bill Williams Mountain.

Total Distance: 4 miles. Your ride can be lengthened via connecting trails.

Location: Williams

Type of Trail: Equestrian/Hiker

Connecting Trails: Bixler Saddle Trail #72, Benham Trail #38

Difficulty: Moderate

Elevation: 7,000 to 9,200 feet

Best Months: Spring through fall

Maps: Kaibab National Forest USGS: Bill Williams Mountain

Trailhead: From downtown Williams, travel west on Railroad Avenue 1 mile. Turn left at the sign indicating Williams Ranger District. Proceed along the frontage road and turn left at the turnoff for the Williams Ranger District office. The trailhead is signed.

BENHAM TRAIL #38

Highlights: An enjoyable trail to the summit of Bill Williams Mountain.

Total Distance: 4.5 miles. Your ride can be lengthened via connecting trails.

Location: Williams

Type of Trail: Equestrian/Hiker

Connecting Trails: Bixler Saddle Trail #72, Bill Williams Mountain Trail #21

Difficulty: Moderate

Elevation: 7,265 to 9,258 feet

Best Months: Spring through fall

Maps: Kaibab National Forest USGS: Bill Williams Mountain

Special Considerations: No water, but toilet facilities available.

Trailhead: From Williams, travel south on 4th Street (the Perkinsville Road and FR 173) about 3.5 miles. Turn right (west) on FR 140. The trailhead is signed and is 0.3 mile from the main road.

OVERLAND ROAD HISTORIC TRAIL #113

Highlights: Along this historic trail are remnants of an old stage
   station and Civilian Conservation Corps (CCC) camps. The trail
   is marked with blazes and rock cairns.

Total Distance: 25 miles

Location: Williams

Type of Trail: Equestrian/Hiker/Mountain Biker

Difficulty: Moderate

Elevation: 5,900 to 7,000 feet

Best Months: Spring through late fall

Maps: Kaibab National Forest USGS: Bill Williams Mountain,
   Garland Prairie

Special Considerations: Mountain bikers use sections of the trail.
   Vehicles may use the trail for a forest road. A forest map would be
   useful in this area. The trail may be hard to find in areas.

Trailhead: There are several trailheads. Here are two: From Williams,
   travel south on the Perkinsville Road (FR 173). Within about 7 miles,
   turn left on FR 139 (Rosilda Springs Road) and drive about 1 mile to
   the trailhead. Signage is on the right side of the road. Or, continue on
   FR 173, and do not turn on FR 139. About 11 miles from Williams,
   FR 173 forks. Take the dirt road, FR 354, about 2 miles to FR 57 and the
   trailhead on the right. This section of the trail is the Old Sheep Trail.

SYCAMORE RIM TRAIL #45

Highlights: A new trail born in 1975, with five trailhead accesses.

Total Distance: 11 miles

Location: Sycamore Canyon Wilderness

Type of Trail: Equestrian/Hiker/Mountain biker

Difficulty: Moderate

Elevation: 6,000 to 6,900 feet

Best Months: Early spring to late fall

Maps: Kaibab National Forest USGS: Bill Williams Mountain,
   Sycamore Point

Special Considerations: There are mountain bikers outside the
   wilderness area. The Pomeroy Tank and Sycamore Falls areas
   are very difficult for horses because of the rocky areas.

Trailhead: From Williams, travel east on I-40 to the Garland Prairie exit (167). Turn right (south) on FR 141 just off the exit and continue for 12 miles. Turn right (southeast) on FR 56. Continue on FR 56 about 1.5 miles to the trailhead parking area.

BIXLER SADDLE TRAIL #72

Highlights: This connecting trail offers a pleasant ride.
Total Distance: 2 miles. Your ride can be lengthened via connecting trails.
Location: Williams
Type of Trail: Equestrian/Hiker
Connecting Trails: Bill Williams Mountain Trail #21, Benham Trail #38
Difficulty: Moderate
Elevation: 7,700 to 8,740 feet
Best Months: Spring through fall
Maps: Kaibab National Forest USGS: Bill Williams Mountain
Special Considerations: No water is available. You will need to purchase a forest map, as this trail does not appear on topo maps.
Trailhead: From Williams, travel west on I-40 to the Devil Dog exit (157). Turn south on FR 108 and travel about 1 mile to FR 45. Turn left (east) and travel about 2 miles to the trailhead. The last half of FR 45 may be a rough road.

KENDRICK MOUNTAIN TRAIL #22

Highlights: An old lookout cabin, built in 1912, sits just below the summit. Great views of the Grand Canyon to the north and Oak Creek Canyon to the South.
Total Distance: 4 miles
Location: Kendrick Mountain Wilderness
Type of Trail: Equestrian/Hiker
Difficulty: Moderate
Elevation: 7,700 to 10,418 feet
Best Months: Late spring through fall
Maps: Kaibab National Forest USGS: Moritz Ridge, Kendric

Trailhead: From Williams, travel east on I-40 to the Parks exit (178). Turn left and cross the overpass. Turn left at the T intersection. Proceed to the Parks store and turn right on FR 141. Continue north about 8 miles. Turn right on FR 194 and travel about 4.5 miles to FR 171. Turn right and travel 2 miles to FR 190. Turn left and travel 1 mile to the trailhead.

Pumpkin Trail #39

Highlights: Parts of this trail (the upper three-quarters) follow an old sheepherders' trail. Remains of an old cabin are alongside the trail about 0.25 mile from the top.
Total Distance: 5.5 miles (one way)
Location: Kendrick Mountain Wilderness
Type of Trail: Equestrian/Hiker
Difficulty: Moderate
Elevation: 7,260 to 10,418 feet
Best Months: Late spring through early fall
Maps: Kaibab National Forest USGS: Moritz Ridge
Special Considerations: A forest map would be helpful.
Trailhead: From Williams, travel east on I-40 to the Parks exit (178). Turn left and cross the overpass. Turn left at the T intersection. Turn right at the Parks store (FR 141) and travel about 11 miles. Turn north on FR 144 and go about 2.5 miles to FR 171. Turn right and go 2.8 miles to the right-angle turn in the road. There, turn left (east) on FR 149, just south of the curve. Continue 1 mile to the trailhead and parking area.

Bull Basin Trail #40 with Connector Trail #80

Highlights: This trail goes through the forest area that was severely burned in the summer of 2000 and is now healing itself. Old Kendrick Cabin still stands, unharmed by the fire. Be sure to visit the lookout tower.
Total Distance: 4.5 miles (Trail #40), 1 miles (Trail #80)
Location: Williams Area

Type of Trail: Equestrian/Hiker
Difficulty: Moderate
Elevation: 8,000 to 10,418 feet
Best Months: Late spring through early fall
Maps: Kaibab National Forest USGS: Moritz Ridge–Kendrick
Trailhead: From Williams, go east on I-40 to the Parks exit (178).
   Turn north and go across the overpass. At the T intersection, turn
   left (west). At the Parks store, turn north on FR 141. Continue
   11 miles to FR 144. Turn north and travel 4 miles to FR 90. Turn
   right and proceed 5 miles to the junction with FR 90A. Turn right
   and follow FR 90A to the trailhead, which is near private land.

North Kaibab Ranger District

EAST RIM TRAIL #7

Highlights: A connecting trail to North Canyon Trail #4.
Total Distance: 1.5 miles
Location: Saddle Mountain Wilderness
Type of Trail: Equestrian/Hiker
Connecting Trails: North Canyon Trail #4
Difficulty: Difficult
Elevation: 8,810 to 6,130 feet
Best Months: Late spring through early fall
Maps: Kaibab National Forest USGS: De Motte
Special Considerations: Purchase a map at the visitor center, as this
  trail does not appear on the topo maps. Experienced riders with
  experienced trail horses only, because of the narrow, steep-sided
  passages.
Trailhead: AZ 67 closes after the first snowfall. From the North
  Kaibab Visitor Center, travel south on AZ 67 26.5 miles. At 0.7 mile
  beyond the De Motte Campground entrance, turn east on FR 611.
  Pass the intersection of FR 610 and continue 2.6 miles to the East
  Rim viewpoint, where the trail starts at the forest boundary.

NORTH CANYON TRAIL #4

Highlights: This trail descends into North Canyon where a perennial
  stream flows. There are multiple stream crossings.
Total Distance: 7 miles
Location: Saddle Mountain Wilderness
Type of Trail: Equestrian/Hiker
Connecting Trails: East Rim Trail #7
Difficulty: Difficult
Elevation: 8,800 to 6,130 feet
Best Months: Late spring to early fall
Maps: Kaibab National Forest USGS: De Motte Park
Special Considerations: Purchase a Forest Service map at the visitor
  center, as this trail does not appear on the topo maps. Experienced

riders with experienced trail horses only, because of the narrow,
steep drop-off passages. AZ 67 closes after the first snowfall.

Trailhead: Travel from the North Kaibab Visitor Center south on
AZ 67 26.5 miles to 0.7 mile beyond the De Motte Campground
entrance. Drive east on FR 611 about 2.7 miles to the trailhead.

JUMPUP-NAIL TRAIL #8

Highlights: This trail passes through narrow, steep-sided areas and
through rugged rock formations as it reaches Sowats Canyon. This
canyon is a popular access to the Colorado River.

Total Distance: 6 miles. Your ride can be lengthened via connecting
trails.

Location: Kaibab Creek Wilderness

Type of Trail: Equestrian/Hiker

Connecting Trails: Ranger Trail (to Kaibab Creek)

Difficulty: Difficult

Elevation: 6,170 to 3,500 feet

Best Months: Spring through fall

Maps: Kaibab National Forest USGS: Big Springs, Jumpup Canyon

Special Considerations: Purchase a Forest Service map at the visitor
center, as this trail is not on the topo map. Experienced riders and
trail horses only. Limited water. High summer temperatures and
very rugged country. AZ 67 closes after the first snowfall.

Trailhead: From the North Kaibab Visitor Center, travel 0.25 miles
south on AZ 67. Turn west on FR 461. Continue on FR 461,
which becomes FR 462, about 9 miles to FR 422. Turn south and
go 11.5 miles (5 miles beyond Big Springs). Turn west on FR 425.
Proceed 8 miles and turn right on FR 233. Follow FR 233 about
9 miles to the trailhead. The road ends 0.5 mile farther at Sowats
Benchmark.

LOOKOUT CANYON TRAIL #120

Highlights: An easy ride that is cool in the summer.

Total Distance: 9 miles

Location: North Kaibab, Kaibab Plateau

Type of Trail: Equestrian/Hiker
Connecting Trails: Lookout Canyon Trail #122
Difficulty: Easy
Elevation: 7,350 to 8,300 feet
Best Months: Late Spring through fall
Maps: Kaibab National Forest USGS: Big Springs, Timp Point, De Motte Park
Special Considerations: There is no water on the trail. AZ 67 is closed after the first snowfall.
Trailhead: From the Kaibab Plateau Visitor Center at Jacob Lake, drive south on AZ 67 0.3 miles to Forest Development Road (FDR) 461. Turn right and drive 6 miles to FDR 462. Continue 3 miles to FDR 22. Turn left and travel about 7 miles to the intersection with FDR 429. Turn right and drive about 0.25 mile to FDR 226. Turn right to reach the trailhead.

SNAKE GULCH-KANAB CREEK TRAIL #59

Highlights: The Snake Gulch Trail winds past multicolored cliffs, pictographs, and a few old homesteads. When this trail joins Kanab Creek, it follows the riparian area, eventually becoming Ranger Trail #41 as it leaves Kanab Creek.
Total Distance: 21.5 miles
Location: Kanab Creek Wilderness
Type of Trail: Equestrian/Hiker
Connecting Trails: Ranger Trail #41
Difficulty: Easy
Elevation: 5,860 to 3,200 feet
Best Months: Spring through early summer, fall through early winter
Maps: Kaibab National Forest USGS: Big Springs, Jumpup Canyon
Special Considerations: Purchase a forest map at the visitor center, as this trail is not on the topo map. Hot in the summer. Extremely remote and rugged country with little water. Check with the visitor center for current information. AZ 67 closes after first snowfall.
Trailhead: From the North Kaibab Visitor Center, travel 0.25 mile south on AZ 67. Turn west on FR 461. Continue on FR 461, which

becomes FR 462, 9 miles to the intersection with FR 422. Turn
south and travel 2 miles to FR 423. Travel west on FR 423 1.3 miles
to FR 642. Turn north and go 2 miles to the terminus of the road
and the trailhead.

RANGER TRAIL #41

Highlights: Towering cliffs hug this remote and rugged trail.
Total Distance: 17 miles. Your ride can be lengthened via connecting
  trails.
Location: Kaibab Creek Wilderness
Type of Trail: Equestrian/Hiker
Connecting Trails: Snake Creek–Kanab Creek Trail #59
Difficulty: Moderate
Elevation: 5,380 to 3,500 feet
Best Months: Spring through early winter
Maps: Kaibab National Forest USGS: Big Springs, Jumpup Canyon
Special Considerations: Purchase a forest map at the visitor center, as
  this trail is not on the topo maps. Water is limited. Very hot in the
  summer. AZ 66 is closed after the first snowfall.
Trailhead: From the North Kaibab Visitor Center, travel south on
  AZ 67 about 0.25 mile. Turn west on FR 461. Continue on FR 461,
  which becomes FR 462, about 9 miles to FR 422. Turn south and
  travel 2 miles to FR 423. Turn right and go 3.3 miles to FR 235.
  Turn right and go 7 miles; this road again becomes FR 423 headed
  southwest. Follow FR 423 about 8 miles, where it ends at Jumpup
  Cabin and the trailhead.

NAVAJO TRAIL #19

Highlights: An old sheepherding and Indian trail. In 1871, John D.
  Lee traversed this area by way of a well-used horse path. He may
  have been the first Anglo to use the Navajo Trail. This trail connects
  to the Kaibab Plateau Trail, which is part of the Arizona Trail.
Total Distance: 12 miles
Location: Kaibab Plateau
Type of Trail: Equestrian/Hiker

Connecting Trails: Kaibab Plateau Trail
Difficulty: Moderate
Elevation: 6,800 to 5,200 feet
Best Months: Spring through early summer, fall through early winter
Maps: Kaibab National Forest USGS: Houserock Spring.
Special Considerations: Purchase a forest map at the visitor center, as the trail is not on the topo map.
Trailhead: There are three access points. Here are two: From the North Kaibab Visitor Center, travel west on US 89A 2 miles. Turn north on FR 248. Continue 11 miles to Joe's Reservoir and the trailhead. Or, from the North Kaibab Visitor Center, travel east on US 89A about 11 miles to about 0.5 mile east of the forest boundary. Turn north at the abandoned gas station. Travel 7 miles to the Two Mile Ranch. The trailhead is on the west side of the road.

NANKOWEAP TRAIL #57

Highlights: The original trail was blazed in 1881 by John Wesley Powell and C. D. Walcott.
Total Distance: 4 miles. Your ride can be lengthened via connecting trails.
Location: North Kaibab, Kaibab Plateau, Saddle Mountain Wilderness
Type of Trail: Equestrian/Hiker
Connecting Trails: Grand Canyon Nankoweap Trail. Saddle Mountain Trail #31
Difficulty: Difficult
Elevation: 8,800 to 6,480 feet
Best Months: Spring through early winter
Maps: Kaibab National Forest USGS: Nankoweap
Special Considerations: Purchase a forest map at the visitor center, as this trail is not on the topo map. It is for experienced trail horses only. AZ 67 is closed after the first snowfall.
Trailhead: In summer through fall, from the North Kaibab Visitor Center, travel south on AZ 67 26.5 miles to 0.7 mile beyond the De Motte Park Campground. Turn east on FR 611 and go about 1.4 miles. Turn south on FR 610 and travel 12.3 miles to where the

road ends at the trailhead (elevation 8,800 feet). In winter through spring, from the North Kaibab Visitor Center, travel east on US 89A about 20 miles. Turn south on FR 445 and go 27 miles. When FR 445 forks, stay right and proceed to the trailhead.

SADDLE MOUNTAIN TRAIL #31

Highlights: A wilderness ride with great views.
Total Distance: 6 miles. You can lengthen your ride via connecting trails.
Location: North Kaibab, Kaibab Plateau, Saddle Mountain Wilderness
Type of Trail: Equestrian/Hiker
Connecting Trails: Nankoweap Trail #57
Difficulty: Easy
Elevation: 7,000 to 6,560 feet
Best Months: Year-round
Maps: Kaibab National Forest USGS: Nankoweap
Special Considerations: Purchase a forest map at the visitor center, as this trail is not on the topo map. No water. High summer temperatures.
Trailhead: From the North Kaibab Visitor Center, travel east on US 89A about 20 miles. Turn south on FR 445. Proceed 27 miles. Stay right at the fork in the road. This takes you to the wilderness boundary and the trailhead.

PRATT CANYON TRAIL #121

Highlights: Part of the Lookout Canyon connecting trail system.
Total Distance: 2.5 miles. Your ride can be lengthened via connecting trails.
Location: North Kaibab, Kaibab Plateau
Type of Trail: Equestrian/Hiker
Connecting Trails: Lookout Canyon Trail #120
Difficulty: Easy
Elevation: 7,350 to 8,300 feet
Best Months: Late spring through early fall

Maps: Kaibab National Forest USGS: Big Springs, Timp Point, De Motte Park

Special Considerations: There is no water. AZ 67 is closed after the first snowfall.

Trailhead: From the Kaibab Plateau Visitor Center at Jacob Lake, drive south on AZ 67 0.3 mile to FDR 461. Turn right and drive 6 miles to FDR 462. Turn left and go 3 miles to FDR 22. Turn left and drive 8 miles to the trailhead, which is on the left.

LOOKOUT CANYON TRAIL #122

Highlights: Part of the connecting trail system of Lookout Canyon.

Total Distance: 1.25 miles. Your ride can be lengthened via connecting trails.

Location: Kaibab Plateau

Type of Trail: Equestrian/Hiker

Connecting Trails: Lookout Canyon Trail #120

Difficulty: Easy

Elevation: 7,350 to 8,300 feet

Best Months: Late spring though fall

Maps: Kaibab National Forest USGS: Timp Point, De Motte Park

Special Considerations: There is no water. AZ 67 is closed after the first snowfall.

Trailhead: From the Kaibab Plateau Visitor Center at Jacob Lake, drive south on AZ 67 0.3 mile to FDR 461. Turn right and drive 6 miles to FDR 462. Turn left and go 3 miles to FDR 22. Turn left and proceed 10.5 miles to the trailhead. At about 8 miles you will pass the trailhead to Pratt Canyon Trail #121.

KAIBAB PLATEAU TRAIL (ARIZONA TRAIL)

Highlights: The oldest segment of the Arizona Trail.

Total Distance: 50.5 miles

Location: North Kaibab Plateau

Type of Trail: Equestrian/Hiker

Difficulty: Moderate

Elevation: 6,500 to 9,000 feet

Best Months: Spring through fall

Maps: Kaibab National Forest USGS: Buck Pasture Canyon, Cooper Ridge, Jacob Lake, De Motte Park

Special Considerations: AZ 67 closes after the first snowfall. For more information, contact the Kaibab Plateau Visitor Center at HC 64, Jacob Lake, AZ 86022, or the Tusayan Ranger District (see page 119).

Trailhead: There are five developed trailheads. For the one on US 89A, from the Kaibab Plateau Visitor Center, drive east on AZ 67 to the junction of US 89A and FDR 205. This is the trailhead. Or, from the Kaibab Plateau Visitor Center, drive south on AZ 67 9 miles to FDR 205. Turn left and drive 0.3 mile to the trailhead. For the East Rim trailhead, from the Kaibab Plateau Visitor Center, drive south on AZ 67 27.5 miles to FDR 611. Turn left and drive 4.4 miles to the trailhead. For the south boundary trailhead, from the Kaibab Plateau Visitor Center, drive south on AZ 67 27.5 miles to FDR 611. Turn left and drive 1.4 miles to FDR 610. Turn right and drive 6 miles to the trailhead. The north boundary trailhead is located at the intersection of FR 248 and the forest boundary 13.5 miles north of US 89A, about 15.5 miles from Jacob Lake. Follow US 89A past Jacob Lake and turn right on FR 248. The trailhead is there.

Tusayan Ranger District

ARIZONA TRAIL (COCONINO RIM VIA RUSSELL WASH TO MOQUI STAGE STATION)

Highlights: Forested trail interspersed with meadows.
Total Distance: 24.2 miles (2 segments of 12 miles each)
Location: Kaibab National Forest
Type of Trail: Equestrian/Hiker/Mountain Biker
Difficulty: Easy to moderate
Elevation: 6,900 to 7,500 feet
Best Months: Year-round
Maps: Kaibab National Forest USGS: De Motte, Jacob Lake;
    Tusayan Ranger District, Arizona Trail Map
Special Considerations: Generally, no water is available.
Trailhead: There are two access points to this trail from the north.
    Access is reached from AZ 64/US 180 in Tusayan. Turn east on
    FR 302, which is 0.8 mile north of the Grand Canyon Airport.
    Continue for 16 miles, following the signs to Grandview Lookout.
    The other northern access is from Grand Canyon National Park.
    From the south entrance station, drive north 4 miles to AZ 64.
    Turn right (east) and drive about 8.7 miles. You will see a Grandview
    Lookout sign on your left. Continue east on AZ 64 2 miles. At the
    Arizona Trail sign, turn right on FR 310 and go 1.3 miles to the
    trailhead and the Grandview Lookout trailhead tower. To access
    the Moqui Stage Stop to Russell Wash segment, from Williams
    travel north on AZ 64 40 miles. Turn right (east) on FR 320 (high
    clearance vehicles only), and continue about 20 miles to FR 301.
    Turn right and go south to the Moqui Stage Stop trailhead.

Prescott National Forest

THE PRESCOTT NATIONAL FOREST was established in 1895 to protect the heavily mined and logged mountains surrounding the city of Prescott. It is half on the east and half on the west of Prescott. After establishment of the original Prescott National Forest, the Verde National Forest was added to protect the valuable watershed of the Verde Valley.

Today the national forest is 1,250,000 acres of wilderness. Elevation ranges from 2,800 feet to the 8,000-foot Mt. Union. The Prescott National Forest is home to Sycamore Canyon, known as the Little Grand Canyon, a great area to ride or hike. The Bradshaw Mountains, located to the south and east of Prescott, compose one of the most mineralized mountain ranges in the world.

Prescott National Forest Trails

Bradshaw Ranger District
Prescott National Forest
Bradshaw Ranger District
2230 E. Highway 69
Prescott, AZ 86301-5657
928-771-4700

Nearby Cities
Prescott, Mayer, Cordes Junction, Cleator, Dewey

Chino Valley Ranger District
Prescott National Forest
Chino Valley Ranger District
PO Box 485
735 N. Highway 89
Chino Valley, AZ 86323-0485
928-636-2302

Nearby Cities
Chino Valley, Clarkdale,
Prescott, Prescott Valley

Verde Ranger District
Prescott National Forest
Verde Ranger District
PO Box 670
Camp Verde, AZ 86322-0670
928-567-4121

Nearby Cities
Camp Verde, Prescott, Cottonwood, Flagstaff, Sedona

Bradshaw Ranger District

WEST SPRUCE TRAIL #264

Highlights: A scenic trail through areas of mining exploration in the high peaks of the Sierra Prieta Range.

Total Distance: 7.4 miles

Location: Prescott

Type of Trail: Equestrian/Hiker

Difficulty: Moderate

Elevation: 7,000 to 5,000 feet

Best Months: Fall through spring

Maps: Prescott National Forest USGS: Iron Spring

Special Considerations: Very hot in the summer.

Trailhead: This trail is divided into two sections. For access to the southern end of the northern section, from Prescott travel west on the Iron Spring Road 6 miles to the turnoff to the Highland Pines development (Skyline Drive). Turn left (south) and follow Skyline Drive about 3 miles. The road becomes dirt (FR 47); follow this for 0.5 mile to the signed area indicating trailhead 0.4 mile ahead. For the southern section, from Prescott, travel west on Gurley Street 2 miles to the Thumb Butte Road. Turn right (north) toward the Thumb Butte Recreation Area. Pass the picnic area at 1 mile. Stay left of the turn to Alma Camp. Continue 0.6 mile to FR 373. Turn left and travel south 3.1 miles. The road makes a horseshoe-shaped turn and the trailhead is to the right of the cattle guard.

GROOM CREEK LOOP TRAIL #307

Highlights: This well-maintained trail is one of the most scenic alternative trails in the Prescott National Forest. Groom Creek Horse Camp is just south of Groom Creek.

Total Distance: 8.7 miles

Location: Bradshaw Mountains

Type of Trail: Equestrian/Hiker

Difficulty: Moderate

Elevation: 6,400 to 7,700 feet

Best Months: March through November
Maps: Prescott National Forest USGS: Groom Creek
Trailhead: Access from the Groom Creek trailhead. From Prescott, travel south on Senator Highway 6.5 miles to Groom Creek. You will pass the entrance (FR 52) to Goldwater Lake.

E Cross L Trail #281

Highlights: One of the finest horseback trails in the Prescott National Forest. Several historical sites. Old Palace Station (now a Forest Service Administration site) served as a stage stop until 1910. Old mines and signs of human habitation in the Ash Creek drainage.
Total Distance: 4.8 miles
Location: Bradshaw Mountains
Type of Trail: Equestrian/Hiker
Difficulty: Moderate
Elevation: 7,000 to 6,100 feet
Best Months: Year-round
Maps: Prescott National Forest USGS: Battleship Butte, Groom Creek
Special Considerations: Hot in summer. Undependable water sources along the trail.
Trailhead: From Prescott, travel south on Senator Highway (FR 52) about 11 miles. Pass the turnoff to Mt. Union (FR 261). At 0.3 mile farther, turn left on FR 52B and go 0.3 mile to FR 81. Travel south on FR 81 another 0.3 mile to where the road meets FR 70. Take FR 70 southeast along the Ash Creek Ridge about 0.4 mile to the trailhead on the right, which is probably not signed.

Algonquin Trail #225

Highlights: This trail is named for the Algonquin Mine, which was established in the early 1900s, and passes by the mine site.
Total Distance: 5 miles
Location: Castle Creek Wilderness
Type of Trail: Equestrian/Hiker
Difficulty: Moderate
Elevation: 6,800 to 4,600 feet

Best Months: Year-round

Maps: Prescott National Forest USGS: Crown King

Special Considerations: May be hot in the summer. Due to high
elevation, snowfields may exist. Campsites along the trail at
0.75 mile and just beyond the abandoned cabin sites farther along
the trail.

Trailhead: Two access points. For the south trailhead, from Prescott,
take AZ 69 to Mayer. In Mayer, take Main Street through town
leading east to the junction with the Antelope Creek Road. Travel
southeast on the Antelope Creek Road 9 miles to Cordes. At the
road junction in Cordes, turn left on FR 259 and go to Crown
King. At Crown King, go south on FR 259A 0.5 mile to FR 52.
Turn left and go 2.2 miles to the Algonquin Trail turnoff. The trailhead is to the southeast 100 yards north of the turnoff. For the
south trailhead, from Phoenix, travel north on I-17 to the Bumble
Bee exit. Take the dirt road north to Bumblebee, then continue on
FR 259 to Crown King. Proceed on FR 259A as above. For the
north trailhead, from Phoenix, travel north on I-17 to the Bumble
Bee exit. Take the dirt road north to Bumblebee. In Bumblebee,
take FR 259 to Cleator. From Cleator continue on FR 259 9.5 miles
to the Poland Vista Point, which is about 2.5 miles from Crown
King. A small parking area is available. The trailhead (unmarked)
begins 100 feet southeast of the parking lot.

GRANITE BASIN RECREATION AREA

Highlights: Equestrians may use trails within the Granite Basin
Recreation Area, which is within 10 miles west of Prescott.

Clark Spring Trail #40	**Total Distance:** 1.8 miles **Difficulty:** Moderate
Mint Wash Trail #345	**Total Distance:** 4.2 miles **Difficulty:** Moderate
Willow Connector Trail #346	**Total Distance:** 0.5 mile **Difficulty:** Easy
Willow Trail #347	**Total Distance:** 6.8 miles **Difficulty:** Moderate

Chimbley Water Trail #348   **Total Distance:** 1.2 miles
                                 Difficulty: Moderate
Balancing Rock Trail #349   **Total Distance:** 3.2 miles
                                 Difficulty: Moderate
West Lake Trail #351   **Total Distance:** 1.5 miles
                                 Difficulty: Moderate
Mint Wash Connector Trail #352 **Total Distance:** 1.2 miles
                                 Difficulty: Moderate

Maps: There is a map board at the Cayuse Day Area that shows how the trails interconnect.

Special Considerations: Horses are restricted to the trails and the Cayuse Day Area and are not allowed at Granite Basin Lake or any other developed sites. For additional information, contact Bradshaw Ranger District, 344 S. Cortez Street, Prescott, AZ 86303-4398, 928-443-8000.

Trailhead: From the courthouse in downtown Prescott, turn right on Montezuma. Continue about 3 miles as Montezuma becomes Iron Spring Road. Continue another 1.5 to 2 miles and, after the Williamson Valley Road, turn right on Granite Basin Road (FR 374). Proceed about 2 miles to the Cayuse Equestrian Day Use Area.

Chino Valley Ranger District

PACKARD MESA TRAIL #66

Highlights: An access trail to Sycamore Canyon.

Total Distance: 5 miles. Your ride can be lengthened via connecting trails.

Location: Cottonwood-Clarkdale, Sycamore Canyon Wilderness

Type of Trail: Equestrian/Hiker

Connecting Trails: Sycamore Trail #63

Difficulty: Moderate

Elevation: 3,700 to 4,900 feet

Best Months: Year-round

Maps: Prescott National Forest USGS: Clarkdale, Sycamore Basin

Special Considerations: Very hot in the summer. If you ride north on Sycamore Trail #63, you will find water for horses at the Sycamore Tank, 0.5 mile north of the junction with Trail #66.

Trailhead: From Clarkdale, travel north on AZ 260 to the Tuzigoot Monument. Immediately after crossing the Verde River bridge, turn left and follow the road that parallels the river. This road becomes FR 131. Follow this road about 10 miles to the Sycamore Canyon overlook just east of the Packard Ranch. You may want to park in this area and ride the final 3 miles to the trailhead, as the gate to the wilderness area will probably be locked.

CEDAR CREEK TRAIL #53

Highlights: This trail is used mainly by horseback riders for access to the Sycamore Canyon Wilderness.

Total Distance: 4.2 miles. Your ride can be lengthened via connecting trails.

Location: Sycamore Canyon Wilderness

Type of Trail: Equestrian/Hiker

Connecting Trails: Sycamore Trail #63

Difficulty: Easy

Elevation: 4,800 to 4,500 feet

Best Months: Spring, fall, and winter

Maps: Prescott National Forest USGS: Sycamore Canyon Basin

Special Considerations: Very hot in the summer. Water for human consumption is not available. Horses may water at the Sycamore Tank, about 0.5 mile south of the junction with Sycamore Trail #63.

Trailhead: From Chino Valley, take the Perkinsville Road (FR 354) north about 23 miles to FR 181. Turn east and go about 6 miles to Henderson Flat and the trailhead. If you want to continue on FR 181, you will need a high clearance vehicle.

YEW THICKET TRAIL #52

Highlights: This trail is entirely in the Sycamore Canyon Wilderness

Total Distance: 5.3 miles

Location: Sycamore Canyon Wilderness

Type of Trail: Equestrian/Hiker

Connecting Trails: Sycamore Trail #63, Lonesome Pocket Trail #61

Difficulty: Moderate

Elevation: 6,400 to 4,500 feet

Best Months: Year-round

Maps: Prescott National Forest USGS: Sycamore Basin

Special Considerations: Very hot in the summer. The upper portion may be difficult to access in the winter due to snowfields. No water is available.

Trailhead: From Williams, travel south on 4th Street to Perkinsville and go past Perkinsville Road (FR 173) about 9 miles to FR 354. Travel south 6 miles to Pine Flats. Turn right on FR 105 and go 1.5 miles to FR 125. You may want to ride to the trailhead, as the last 6 miles of FR 125 are very tough going. Or, from Chino Valley, travel north on the Perkinsville Road (FR 354) past Perkinsville to FR 181. Proceed east to Henderson Flat. Mount up and proceed to the trail junction.

SYCAMORE TRAIL #63

Highlights: This is the main access trail to the Sycamore Canyon Wilderness. Two historic cabins (Winter and Taylor) can be reached from this trail.

Total Distance: 11.2 miles. Your ride can be lengthened via connecting trails.

Location: Sycamore Canyon Wilderness

Type of Trail: Equestrian/Hiker

Connecting Trails: Railroad Draw Trail #68, Yew Thicket Trail #52, Trail #117, and Winter Cabin Trail #70

Difficulty: Moderate

Elevation: 4,600 to 6,500 feet

Best Months: Year-round

Maps: Prescott National Forest USGS: Sycamore Basin, Loy Butte, Sycamore Point

Special Considerations: It is very hot in the summer. Some snowfields may exist near Winter Cabin in the winter.

Trailhead: The best approach is from Chino Valley. From Chino Valley, travel north on the Perkinsville Road (FR 354) about 23 miles to FR 181. Turn east and go about 6 miles to Henderson Flat. Continue southeast for an additional 5 miles to the Wilderness Boundary. Or, from Prescott, travel north on AZ 89 toward Ash Fork 25–30 miles to FR 492. Turn right (east) and go 11 miles to FR 354. Turn south and go 2 miles to FR 181. Turn east and go 6 miles to Henderson Flat. It is 5 miles farther to the Sycamore Canyon Boundary.

RAILROAD DRAW TRAIL #68

Highlights: Mainly a cattle trail.

Total Distance: 3 miles. Your ride can be lengthened via connecting trails.

Location: Sycamore Canyon Wilderness

Type of Trail: Equestrian/Hiker

Connecting Trails: Sycamore Trail #63, Packard Mesa Trail #66

Difficulty: Moderate to easy

Elevation: 3,800 to 4,500 feet

Best Months: Year-round

Maps: Prescott National Forest USGS: Clarkdale, Sycamore Basin

Special Considerations: Very hot in the summer. There is no water.

Trailhead: From Clarkdale, travel north on AZ 260 to the Tuzigoot Monument Road. Continue on AZ 260 and cross the Verde River bridge. Turn left immediately after the bridge and travel this road paralleling the river. This road becomes FR 131. Proceed about 10 miles to the Sycamore Canyon Lookout just east of the Packard Ranch. You may want to ride the final 3 miles to the trailhead, as the gate to the wilderness area will probably be locked.

JUNIPER SPRINGS TRAIL #2

Highlights: A connecting trail to Juniper Mesa Trail #20.
Total Distance: 3.7 miles. Your ride can be lengthened via connecting trails.
Location: Juniper Mesa Wilderness
Type of Trail: Equestrian/Hiker
Connecting Trails: Juniper Mesa Trail #20, Old Military Trail #1, Oaks and Willow Trail #3
Difficulty: Difficult
Elevation: 5,100 to 6,300 feet
Best Months: Year-round
Maps: Prescott National Forest USGS Indian Peak
Special Considerations: This is a steep, difficult trail for experienced mountain horses only.
Trailhead: From Prescott, travel north on the Williamsen Valley Road 38 miles to FR 95. Travel west 1.5 miles to Walnut Creek Station. The trailhead is on FR 95 0.2 mile east of here. The Old Military Trail #1 shares this trailhead.

JUNIPER MESA TRAIL #20

Highlights: With unique views of northern Arizona, this trail offers varied wilderness experiences in a remote area.
Total Distance: 6.5 miles. You can lengthen your ride when using access to this trail via Juniper Springs Trail #2.
Location: Juniper Mesa Wilderness
Type of Trail: Equestrian/Hiker
Connecting Trails: Juniper Springs Trail #2, Old Military Trail #1, Oaks and Willow Trail #3

Difficulty: Easy to difficult
Elevation: 6,200 to 7,000 feet
Best Months: Year-round
Maps: Prescott National Forest USGS: Juniper Mountain, Indian Peak
Special Considerations: For experienced riders and mountain horses only. The western terminus of the trail intersects Oaks and Willow Trail #3, and proceeds down through George Wood Canyon or northeast to Pine Springs FR 7.
Trailhead: Access this trail via the Juniper Springs Trail #2, and the trailhead for Old Military Trail #1. From Prescott, travel north on the Williamson Valley Road 38 miles to FR 95. Travel west for 1.5 miles to Walnut Creek Station. The trailhead is on FR 95 0.2 mile east of here.

OAKS AND WILLOW TRAIL #3

Highlights: This trail travels through George Wood Canyon to the Juniper Mesa Wilderness.
Total Distance: 6.6 miles. You can lengthen your ride via connecting trails.
Location: Juniper Mesa Wilderness
Type of Trail: Equestrian/Hiker
Connecting Trails: Juniper Mesa Trail #20, Pine Creek Drainage Area and FR 7
Difficulty: Moderate to difficult
Elevation: 5,900 to 7,000 feet
Best Months: Year-round
Maps: Prescott National Forest USGS: Juniper Mountain, Indian Peak
Trailhead: From Prescott, travel north on the Williamson Valley Road (FR 6) about 38 miles to FR 95. Turn west and travel 1.5 miles to Walnut Creek Station and FR 150. Travel west on FR 150 6 miles. Proceed only to the locked "Gate Ahead" sign. If you travel farther, you will have difficulty turning around. The trailhead is 0.3 mile past the sign. For the east trailhead, from Prescott, go north on FR 6 about 20 miles to FR 7. Turn left and go 12 miles to the Pine Springs trailhead.

LONESOME POCKET TRAIL #61

Highlights: A connecting trail.

Total Distance: 1.75 miles. Your ride can be lengthened via connecting trails.

Location: Along the Sycamore Canyon Wilderness

Type of Trail: Equestrian/Hiker

Connecting Trails: Cedar Creek Trail #53, Sand Flat Trail #60, Yew Thicket Trail #52

Difficulty: Difficult

Elevation: 4,400 to 6,500 feet

Best Months: Year around

Maps: Prescott National Forest USGS: Sycamore Basin

Special Considerations: Very hot in the summer. A rugged and steep trail in the ascent to the Mogollon Rim.

Trailhead: The trailhead is at Henderson Flat. From Chino Valley, take the Perkins Road (FR 354) about 23 miles to FR 181. Go east about 6 miles to Henderson Flat and the trailhead for Cedar Creek Trail #53. If you want to continue on FR 181, you will need a high clearance vehicle.

OLD MILITARY TRAIL #1

Highlights: A historic military trail that was used to travel from Camp Huolajai to Happy Camp.

Total Distance: 11.7 miles. Your ride can be lengthened via connecting trails.

Location: Along the Juniper Mesa Wilderness (in spots)

Type of Trail: Equestrian/Hiker

Connecting Trails: Juniper Springs Trail #2

Difficulty: Easy

Elevation: 5,200 to 6,100 feet

Best Months: Spring through fall

Maps: Prescott National Forest USGS: Juniper Mountain, Indian Peak, Turkey Canyon

Special Considerations: You may ride this trail to access trails in the Juniper Mesa Wilderness. From the trailhead, near the Walnut

Creek Station, Oak and Willows Trail #3 brings you to Juniper Springs and the junction with Juniper Mesa Trail #20. Or, follow the Old Military Trail from Happy Camp to the intersection with FR 7. Follow FR 7 to Pine Creek, Pine Spring, and the beginning of Oak and Willows Trail #3.

Trailhead: From Prescott, go north on the Williamson Valley Road (FR 6) 38 miles to FR 95. Turn west and drive 1.5 miles; just 0.2 mile beyond the Walnut Creek Work Station is the trailhead. About 0.3 mile north of the trailhead gate, Trail #1 breaks east. Follow the rock cairns and blazes. For the north access, from Prescott, go north on FR 6 (also known as CR 5 or 6) to FR 1 at the Yavapai Ranch Headquarters and the forest boundary. Turn left (west) and continue until you reach Happy Camp.

SAND FLAT TRAIL #60

Highlights: Used mostly by ranchers as a pack trail. It also serves as a connector for other trails entering the Sycamore Canyon Wilderness.

Total Distance: 3.4 miles. Your ride can be lengthened via connecting trails.

Location: Near the Sycamore Canyon Wilderness

Type of Trail: Equestrian/Hiker

Connecting Trails: Lonesome Pocket Trail #61, Yew Thicket Trail #52

Difficulty: Easy

Elevation: 4,400 to 5,500 feet

Best Months: Year around

Maps: Prescott National Forest USGS: Perkinsville, Sycamore Basin

Special Considerations: Hot in the summer. Water is not available.

Trailhead: From Chino Valley, go north on FR 354 past Perkinsville to FR 179, a total of about 25 miles. Turn right and drive 2.5 miles, passing the Pine Flat Ranch. The trailhead is adjacent to the flagstone quarries.

Prescott National Forest: Verde Ranger District

Coconino National Forest: Beaver Creek, Long Valley, and Blue Ridge Ranger Districts

Apache-Sitgreaves National Forest: Chevelon, Heber, and Lakeside Ranger Districts.

GENERAL CROOK TRAIL

Highlights: This famous historic trail, 138 miles long, once served the U.S. Army for moving supplies from Ft. Whipple to Ft. Apache. Due to the length, various national forest districts and ranger districts manage the trail. See pages 2–3 and 52–53 for other addresses to write for information.

Total Distance: 138 miles

Location: From Dewey, the trail heads east through Camp Verde, across the Mogollon Rim, through the Recreation Lakes, and on to Cottonwood Wash in the Pinetop-Lakeside area and Pinedale.

Connecting Trails: Multiple trails

Type of Trail: Equestrian/Hiker

Difficulty: Moderate

Elevation: 3,098 to 7,931 feet

Best Months: Year-round

Maps: National Forest, USGS: Prescott National Forest, Coconino National Forest, and Apache-Sitgreaves National Forest

Trailhead: There are multiple access points; see pages 25, 38, and 69 for the sections you wish to travel.

VIEW POINT TRAIL #106

Highlights: A short connecting trail with great views and fall color.

Total Distance: 1.9 miles. Your ride can be lengthened via connecting trails. This trail forms a loop and makes an attractive, short day ride from Mingus Mountain Campground.

Location: Mingus Mountain Recreation Area

Type of Trail: Equestrian/Hiker

Connecting Trails: North Mingus Trail #105, Trail #105A
Difficulty: Moderate to difficult
Elevation: 7,700 to 6,000 feet
Best Months: Year-round
Maps: Prescott National Forest USGS: Cottonwood
Special Considerations: Can be hot in the summer. Initial descent from the campground could be difficult; use experienced trail horses only.
Trailhead: From Prescott, travel east on AZ 89A. Upon reaching the summit of Mingus Mountain, go south on FR 104 2.6 miles to the Mingus Mountain Campground.

NORTH MINGUS TRAIL #105

Highlights: A pleasant loop trail from the Mingus Mountain Campground.
Total Distance: 4.25 miles. Your ride can be lengthened via connecting trails to complete the loop.
Location: Mingus Mountain and Mescal Spring area
Type of Trail: Equestrian/Hiker
Connecting Trails: View Point Trail #106. Trail #105A
Difficulty: Moderate
Elevation: 7,900 to 6,100 feet
Best Months: Year-round
Maps: Prescott National Forest USGS: Cottonwood, Hickey Mountain
Trailhead: From Prescott, travel east on AZ 89A. Upon reaching the summit of Mingus Mountain, take FR 104 south 2.6 miles to the Mingus Mountain Campground. At the campground, take the left fork to the hang glider site and the trailhead.

PINE FLAT TRAIL #165

Highlights: A connecting trail.
Total Distance: 3.2 miles. Your ride can be lengthened via connecting trails.
Location: Pine Mountain Wilderness

Type of Trail: Equestrian/Hiker
Connecting Trails: Nelson Trail #159
Difficulty: Moderate
Elevation: 5,300 to 6,000 feet
Best Months: Year-round
Maps: Prescott National Forest USGS: Tule Mesa
Trailhead: From Flagstaff, travel south on I-17 and exit at Dugas (FR 68). Travel southeast on FR 68 18 miles to the Nelson Trail trailhead, about 1.25 miles east of the Double T Ranch on Sycamore Creek. Ride 0.8 mile on Nelson Trail #159 from the trailhead to connect with this trail.

VERDE RIM TRAIL #161

Highlights: A fairly level trail with a spectacular view from rugged country.
Total Distance: 5.3 miles. Your ride can be lengthened via connecting trails.
Location: Pine Mountain Wilderness
Type of Trail: Equestrian/Hiker
Connecting Trails: Nelson Trail #159, Willow Spring Trail #12, Pine Flat Trail #165
Difficulty: Difficult
Elevation: 6,400 to 5,900 feet
Best Months: Year-round
Maps: Prescott National Forest USGS: Tule Mesa
Special Considerations: Unpredictable water sources at Willow and Pine Springs. Relatively flat and easy with the exception of the difficult, steep climb up Pine Mountain.
Trailhead: From Flagstaff, travel south on I-17. Exit at Dugas. Go east on FR 68 to FR 68G (high clearance vehicles only). Travel east 8 miles. On Tule Mesa, the road heads southwest then turns east about 0.6 mile past the point where it passes under the power line. Continue on FR 68G as it drops toward the power plant. At FR 9626B, go south 1.1 miles to the Pine Mountain Wilderness boundary and the trailhead.

WILLOW SPRINGS TRAIL #12

Highlights: A connecting trail that provides access to the Pine
Mountain Wilderness.
Total Distance: 1.6 miles. Your ride can be lengthened via connecting
trails.
Location: Pine Mountain Wilderness
Type of Trail: Equestrian/Hiker
Connecting Trails: Nelson Trail #159, Verde Rim #161, Pine Flat
Trail #165
Difficulty: Difficult
Elevation: 7,400 to 6,000 feet
Best Months: Year-round
Maps: Prescott National Forest USGS: Tule Mesa
Special Considerations: Unpredictable water sources at Willow and
Pine Springs.
Trailhead: From Flagstaff, travel south on I-17 and exit at Dugas.
Travel southeast on FR 68 for 18 miles to the Nelson trailhead.
Ride 2.71 miles east on Nelson Trail #159 to connect with Trail #12.

NELSON TRAIL #159

Highlights: A service trail still used to move livestock.
Total Distance: 8.2 miles. Your ride may be lengthened via connect-
ing trails.
Location: Pine Mountain Wilderness
Type of Trail: Equestrian/Hiker
Connecting Trails: Pine Flat Trail #165, Verde Rim Trail #161,
Willow Springs Trail #12
Difficulty: Moderate
Elevation: 5,200 to 6,000 feet
Best Months: Year-round
Maps: Prescott National Forest USGS: Tule Mesa
Special Considerations: May be hot and dry in summer.
Trailhead: From Flagstaff, travel south on I-17 and exit at Dugas.
Travel southeast on FR 68 18 miles to the trailhead (Salt Flat).

OXBOW TRAIL #163

Highlights: Provides access to the Cedar Bench Wilderness.
Total Distance: 5.8 miles. Your ride can be lengthened via connecting
  trails.
Location: Cedar Bench Wilderness
Type of Trail: Equestrian/Hiker
Connecting Trails: Cold Water Trail #27, Chalk Tank Trail #506
Difficulty: Difficult
Elevation: 3,500 to 6,000 feet
Best Months: Year-round
Maps: Prescott National Forest USGS: Tule Mesa, Horner Mountain
Special Considerations: Hot in the summer. The trail terminus is on
  FR 684.
Trailhead: There are two approaches to this trail. For the northern
  trailhead, from Camp Verde, travel south on the Salt Mine Road.
  Just before the bridge, the Salt Mine Road heads west, then turns
  south and becomes FR 574. Travel 14.5 miles to Gap Creek. Park at
  the locked gate and ride 0.3 miles to the Cedar Bench Wilderness
  boundary, where Cold Water Trail #27 begins and leads to Oxbow
  Trail #163, which begins approximately 0.9 mile ahead at Bear
  Grass Tank. For the southern trailhead, exit I-17 at Dugas (FR 69)
  and travel east to Dugas. Just east of town, turn left (east) on FR 686
  and go 5 miles. The trailhead is located at Horse Pasture Tank.

CHASM CREEK TRAIL #164

Highlights: A pleasant trail through the Cedar Bench Wilderness.
Total Distance: 6.1 miles
Location: Cedar Bench Wilderness
Type of Trail: Equestrian/Hiker
Difficulty: Difficult
Elevation: 3,200 to 5,600 feet
Best Months: Year-round
Maps: Prescott National Forest USGS: Arnold Mesa, Horner
  Mountain
Special Considerations: Can be hot in the summer.

Trailhead: From Camp Verde, travel south on the Salt Mine Road about 13 miles before crossing the Verde River bridge. Take the Salt Mine Road west. This road turns south and becomes FR 574. Continue on FR 574 about 10 miles. The trailhead is 0.2 mile north of where the road crosses Chasm Creek.

BLACK CANYON TRAIL #114

Highlights: Panoramic views of Red Rock country and San Francisco Peaks. Multiple connecting trails can be accessed from the Gaddes Canyon trailhead.
Total Distance: 6.6 miles. Your ride can be lengthened via connecting trails as above.
Location: Mingus Mountain area
Type of Trail: Equestrian/Hiker
Difficulty: Moderate
Elevation: 4,100 to 6,400 feet
Best Months: Year-round
Maps: Prescott National Forest USGS: Cottonwood
Special Considerations: Hot in the summer. The trail terminus is at Allen Spring Road.
Trailhead: There are two accesses. From Cottonwood, travel south on AZ 260 4 miles to FR 359. Turn west and travel 4.5 miles to the trailhead at Quail Springs. Or, for the upper west end of the trail, from Clarkdale, travel south on AZ 89A toward Prescott. At the airport, turn left on FR 104, and travel south 5.5 miles to FR 413. Continue south on FR 413 4.5 miles to the trailhead in Gaddes Canyon.

COLD WATER TRAIL #27

Highlights: This historic trail was once used as a military trail between Ft. McDowell and Ft. Lincoln in Camp Verde.
Total Distance: 5.7 miles. Your ride can be lengthened via connecting trails.
Location: Cedar Bench Wilderness
Type of Trail: Equestrian/Hiker

Connecting Trails: Oxbow Trail #163
Difficulty: Difficult
Elevation: 3,000 to 6,300 feet
Best Months: Year-round
Maps: Prescott National Forest USGS: Tule Mesa, Horner Mountain
Special Considerations: The trail terminus is on FR 68G. Hot in the summer.
Trailhead: From Flagstaff, travel south on I-17 and exit at Dugas. Take the Dugas Road (FR 68) toward Dugas. 4 miles east of town, go east on FR 68G 8 miles. The trailhead is 0.25 mile north of the road.

Tonto National Forest

THE TONTO is the largest of Arizona's national forests, with nearly 2.9 million acres and elevations ranging from 1,300 to 8,000 feet. The ecosystems of this forest are varied, as in most of the other national forests of Arizona. They range from Sonoran Desert country to the mixed conifers of higher elevations. Five lakes dot the Tonto. There are two rivers; wild river comprises 22.2 miles of these. Eight wilderness areas add up to 589,300 acres of rough and rugged backcountry. For recreation use, there are about 900 miles of trails.

The Hohokam Indians were the first inhabitants of the area. The U.S. Army eventually removed the Indians and sent them to Ft. Apache and San Carlos. Once the Indians were gone, white settlers, particularly miners and Mormon farmers, settled in the area. Gradually, the Mormon colony withdrew. The building of Roosevelt Dam and the need to protect the Verde and Salt River watersheds led to the creation of the Tonto National Forest in 1905.

Tonto National Forest Trails

Cave Creek Ranger District

Tonto National Forest
Cave Creek Ranger District
40202 N. Cave Creek Road
Scottsdale, AZ 85262
480-595-3300

Nearby Cities
Cave Creek, Scottsdale, Mesa, Payson

Globe Ranger District

Tonto National Forest
Globe Ranger District
Route 1, Box 33
Globe, AZ 85501
928-402-6200

Nearby City
Globe

Mesa Ranger District

Tonto National Forest
Mesa Ranger District
PO Box 5800
Mesa, AZ 85211-5800
480-610-3300

Nearby Cities
Mesa, Apache Junction, Superior

Payson Ranger District
Tonto National Forest
Payson Ranger District
1009 E. Highway 260
Payson, AZ 85541
928-474-7900

Nearby Cities
Payson, Strawberry

Page   Trails
184   Fossil Springs Trail #18
184   Oak Spring Trail #16

Page   Trails
184   Highline Trail #31
185   See Canyon Trail #184

Pleasant Valley Ranger District
Tonto National Forest
Pleasant Valley Ranger District
PO Box 450
Young, AZ 85334
928-462-4300

Nearby Cities
Payson, Strawberry

Page   Trails
186   Deep Creek Trail #128
186   Parker Creek Trail #160
187   Lucky Strike Trail #144
187   Center Mountain Trail #142
188   Grapevine Trail #135
188   Coon Spring Trail #124
189   Coon Creek Trail #254

Page   Trails
189   Rim Trail #139
190   Moody Point Trail #140
191   McFadden Horse Trail #146
191   Bear Flat Trail #178
192   Boyer Trail #148
192   Cienega Trail #145

Cave Creek Ranger District

COTTONWOOD TRAIL #247

Highlights: A pleasant, scenic ride with several stream crossings. Streams are seasonal.

Total Distance: 10.8 miles. Your ride can be lengthened via connecting trails.

Location: Seven Springs Recreation Area

Type of Trail: Equestrian/Hiker

Connecting Trails: Cave Creek Trail #4, Skunk Tank Trail #246, Quien Sabe Trail #250

Difficulty: Difficult

Elevation: 2,480 to 3,920 feet

Best Months: Year-round

Maps: Tonto National Forest USGS: Humboldt Mountain, New River Mesa

Special Considerations: Very hot in the summer. Four-wheel-drive is needed to access Spur Cross trailhead.

Trailhead: There are two points of access. The Cave Creek trailhead is accessed from FR 205, which is an extension of Cave Creek Carefree Road, or from Spur Cross Road. From Cave Creek, travel north on the Spur Cross Road (FR 48) about 6.2 miles to the Spur Cross trailhead.

SKUNK TANK TRAIL #246

Highlights: Scenic views. The trail passes through a burn area.

Total Distance: 4.8 miles. Your ride can be lengthened via connecting trails.

Location: Seven Springs Recreation Area

Type of Trail: Equestrian/Hiker

Connecting Trails: Cottonwood Trail #247, Quien Sabe Trail #250, Cave Creek Trail #4

Difficulty: Difficult

Elevation: 3,440 to 4,080 feet

Best Months: Year-round
Maps: Tonto National Forest USGS: Humboldt Mountain, New
  River Mesa
Special Considerations: Very hot in the summer. No water is available.
Trailhead: From Cave Creek, travel east on the Cave Creek Carefree
  Road about 7.8 miles. Go past FR 205, which is the road to Horse-
  shoe Lake. The paved road ends and becomes FR 24. Follow this
  road 9 miles to the trailhead.

SADDLE RIDGE TRAIL #14

Highlights: This trail crosses the East Verde River near the L-F
  Ranch.
Total Distance: 8 miles. Your ride can be lengthened via connecting
  trails.
Location: Mazatzal Wilderness
Type of Trail: Equestrian/Hiker
Connecting Trails: Bull Spring Trail #34
Difficulty: Moderate
Elevation: 3,240 to 5,800 feet
Best Months: Year-round
Maps: Tonto National Forest, Mazatzal Wilderness
Special Considerations: There is high water at times in the East
  Verde River; crossing can be difficult and dangerous. Water is avail-
  able west of the trail at Carr Spring, Indian Spring, and L.P. Spring.
Trailhead: From Payson, drive west on Main Street (which becomes
  FR 406) about 11 miles. Turn right to the small parking area,
  located about 100 yards beyond the steep switchback. This road
  is very steep and four-wheel-drive vehicles are needed for hauling
  horses and horse trailers.

BULL SPRING TRAIL #34

Highlights: This trail was once a primitive road.
Total Distance: 6.5 miles. Your ride can be lengthened via connecting
  trails.

Location: Mazatzal Wilderness
Type of Trail: Equestrian/Hiker
Connecting Trails: Saddle Ridge Trail #14
Difficulty: Moderate
Elevation: 3,400 to 5,240 feet
Best Months: Year-round
Maps: Tonto National Forest, Mazatzal Wilderness
Special Considerations: Stock water is available at Trail Spring and east of this trail at Oak Thicket Spring (hidden in a bush), Bull Frog Springs, Bull Springs, and Bull Trap Spring.
Trailhead: From Payson, drive west on Main Street, which becomes FR 406. Continue on this road for 12 miles to the end of the road at the trailhead. The road is steep and rough; four-wheel-drive vehicles are recommended. At the trailhead is a private road into the wilderness, which is under lease to a local rancher, and vehicles are not allowed. Park here. Stock water is available.

SOUTH FORK TRAIL #46

Highlights: Travels through an interesting canyon, which offers shade and cool temperatures.
Total Distance: 7.5 miles. Your ride can be lengthened via connecting trail #47.
Location: Mazatzal Wilderness
Type of Trail: Equestrian/Hiker
Connecting Trails: Gold Ridge Trail #47 (motorized vehicles)
Difficulty: Moderate
Elevation: 3,400 to 6,040 feet
Best Months: Year-round
Maps: Tonto National Forest, Mazatzal Wilderness
Special Considerations: Water is available at Pidgeon Springs. Deer Creek Trail #45, which connects to this trail, is not recommended for horses.
Trailhead: From Payson, drive south on AZ 87 to its junction with AZ 188. Across from this intersection, a small road turns off to the left (west). Continue on this road a short distance to the trailhead.

HIGH WATER TRAIL #20

Highlights: This trail follows the Verde River on the east side, hence eliminating two river crossings.
Total Distance: 4.4 miles. Your ride can be lengthened via connecting trails.
Location: Mazatzal Wilderness
Type of Trail: Equestrian/Hiker
Connecting Trails: Wet Bottom Mesa Trail #269, Verde River Trail #11
Difficulty: Moderate
Elevation: 2,080 to 5,900 feet
Best Months: Year-round
Maps: Tonto National Forest, Mazatzal Wilderness
Trailhead: There are two access points to this trail using connecting trails. To access via Verde River Trail #11, from Payson, travel north on AZ 87 about 19 miles to Strawberry. Turn left at the Strawberry Lodge (FR 428) and drive 5 miles to FR 427. Turn left and drive 0.6 mile to FR 194. Turn right and continue 5 miles to the trailhead. This road is steep and rough, and requires four-wheel-drive vehicles. Or, from Payson, drive west on Main Street, which becomes FR 406. Continue on this road for 12 miles to the end of the road at the trailhead. The road is steep and rough; four-wheel-drive vehicles are recommended. At the trailhead is a private road into the wilderness, which is under lease to a local rancher, and vehicles are not allowed. Park here. Stock water is available.

CORNUCOPIA TRAIL #86

Highlights: An old road. The northern aspect of this trail is easy to follow and travel. Some areas may be overgrown.
Total Distance: 3.5 miles. Your ride can be lengthened via connecting trails.
Location: Mazatzal Wilderness
Type of Trail: Equestrian/Hiker
Connecting Trails: Mazatzal Divide Trail #23, Thicket Spring Trail #95
Difficulty: Moderate
Elevation: 4,400 to 5,250 feet
Best Months: Year-round

Maps: Tonto National Forest, Mazatzal Wilderness

Special Considerations: Water is available on Mazatzal Divide Trail #23 at Bear Springs, Chilson Springs, Horse Seep Camp, and Jones Springs.

Trailhead: From Mesa, travel north on AZ 87 about 46 miles to the Slate Creek Divide. Turn left on FR 201. This road serves as a trailhead for many other trails. Unfortunately, the farther you travel, the more difficult it becomes; horse trailers are not recommended. It would be best to ride up FR 201 to the trail you want to ride.

THICKET SPRING TRAIL #95

Highlights: A short connecting side trail off Cornucopia Trail #86

Total Distance: 2 miles. Your ride can be lengthened via connecting trails.

Location: Mazatzal Wilderness

Type of Trail: Equestrian/Hiker

Connecting Trails: Cornucopia Trail #86 to Mazatzal Divide Trail #23

Difficulty: Difficult

Elevation: 4,840 to 5,600 feet

Best Months: Year-round

Maps: Tonto National Forest, Mazatzal Wilderness

Special Considerations: Hot in the summer. There is stock water at Thicket Spring.

Trailhead: There is no direct trailhead access. Connect to one of the other trails or from the Cornucopia Trail at the Peeley trailhead. From Mesa, travel north on AZ 87 about 46 miles to the Slate Creek Divide. Turn left on FR 201. This road serves as a trailhead for many other trails. Unfortunately, the farther you travel, the more difficult it becomes; horse trailers are not recommended. It would be best to ride up FR 201 to the trail you want to ride.

MAZATZAL DIVIDE TRAIL #23

Highlights: A popular, well-laid out-trail for north-south travel.

Total Distance: 27 miles. Your ride can be lengthened via connecting trails.

Location: Mazatzal Wilderness

Type of Trail: Equestrian/Hiker
Connecting Trails: Cornucopia Trail #86, Fisher Trail #230, Sandy
   Saddle Trail #231, Red Hills Trail #262, Brody Seep Trail #264,
   Y Bar Basin Trail #44
Difficulty: Difficult
Elevation: 3,500 to 7,180 feet
Best Months: Year-round
Maps: Tonto National Forest, Mazatzal Wilderness
Special Considerations: Stock water is available at Bear Springs,
   Chilson Springs, Horse Seep Camp, and Jones Spring. Willow
   Spring Trail #223, North Peak Trail #24, Rock Creek Trail #42,
   and Barnhardt Trail #43, which connect to this trail, are not
   recommended for horses.
Trailhead: From Payson, drive west on Main Street (which becomes
   FR 406) about 11 miles. Turn right to the small parking area, which
   is about 100 yards beyond the steep switchback. This road is very
   steep and four-wheel-drive vehicles are needed for hauling horses
   and horse trailers. The trail begins across the road from the trailhead.

SHEEP CREEK TRAIL #88

Highlights: This trail enters a remote area of Mazatzal Wilderness.
Total Distance: 10.6 miles. Your ride can be lengthened via connect-
   ing trails.
Location: Mazatzal Wilderness
Type of Trail: Equestrian/Hiker
Connecting Trails: Davenport Wash Trail #89, Saddle Mountain Trail
   #91
Difficulty: Difficult
Elevation: 3,020 to 5,520 feet
Best Months: Year-round
Maps: Tonto National Forest, Mazatzal Wilderness
Special Considerations: Recommended only for experienced riders
   and horses. Some very steep areas northeast of Squaw Creek. Water
   is not available.
Trailhead: This trail is accessible only from other backcountry trails.
   You can access from Davenport Wash Trail #89, but this requires

fording the Verde River. You can also access from Saddle Mountain Trail #91 by using the Mormon Grove trailhead. From Mesa, drive north on AZ 87 about 46 miles to the Slate Creek Divide. Turn sharply left on Road #25; proceed for 2 miles. Turn up the west fork, go 0.5 mile, and park here. Ride your horse left at the road junction, across the creek, and up the road about 1.5 miles to the trailhead. Corrals are at the end of the road.

SADDLE MOUNTAIN TRAIL #91

Highlights: An interesting and popular trail that is an old prospector road.
Total Distance: 4.5 miles. Your ride can be lengthened via connecting trails.
Location: Mazatzal Wilderness
Type of Trail: Equestrian/Hiker
Connecting Trails: Sheep Creek Trail #88, Davenport Wash Trail #89
Difficulty: Moderate
Elevation: 5,000 to 5,500 feet
Best Months: Year-round
Maps: Tonto National Forest, Mazatzal Wilderness
Special Considerations: Hot in the summer. Water is not available.
Trailhead: This trail is accessible only from other backcountry trails. You can access from Davenport Wash Trail #89, but this requires fording the Verde River. You can also access from Saddle Mountain Trail #91 by using the Mormon Grove trailhead. From Mesa drive north on AZ 87 about 46 miles to the Slate Creek Divide. Turn sharply left on Road #25; proceed for 2 miles. Turn up the west fork, go 0.5 mile, and park here. Ride your horse left at the road junction, across the creek, and up the road about 1.5 miles to the trailhead. Corrals are at the end of the road.

FISHER TRAIL #230

Highlights: A connecting trail.
Total Distance: 3.3 miles. Your ride can be lengthened via connecting trails.
Location: Mazatzal Wilderness

Type of Trail: Equestrian/Hiker
Connecting Trails: Mazatzal Divide Trail #23, Brody Seep Trail #264
Difficulty: Difficult
Elevation: 5,000 to 6,000 feet
Best Months: Year-round
Maps: Tonto National Forest, Mazatzal Wilderness
Special Considerations: For experienced riders and horses only. Parts of the trail are steep and rocky. Water is probably available on Trail #264 at Brody Seep, and on Mazatzal Divide Trail #23 at Bear Springs and Chilson Springs.
Trailhead: No trailhead. Backcountry access only by using Mazatzal Divide Trail #23 at the Peeley trailhead. From Mesa, travel north on AZ 87 about 46 miles to the Slate Creek Divide. Turn left on FR 201. This road serves as a trailhead for many other trails. Unfortunately, the farther you travel, the more difficult it becomes; horse trailers are not recommended. It would be best to ride up FR 201 to the trail you want to ride.

SANDY SADDLE TRAIL #231

Highlights: A connecting trail with long steep grades.
Total Distance: 3 miles. Your ride can be lengthened via connecting trails.
Location: Mazatzal Wilderness
Type of Trail: Equestrian/Hiker
Connecting Trails: Mazatzal Divide Trail #23
Difficulty: Difficult
Elevation: 5,620 to 6,400 feet
Best Months: Year-round
Maps: Tonto National Forest, Mazatzal Wilderness
Special Considerations: For experienced riders and horses only. West to east travel is recommended. Water is probably available at Bear Spring on Mazatzal Divide Trail #23. Barnhardt Trail #43, which connects to this trail, is not recommended for horses.
Trailhead: No trailhead. Backcountry access only by using Mazatzal Divide Trail #23 at the Peeley trailhead. From Mesa, travel north on AZ 87 about 46 miles to the Slate Creek Divide. Turn left on

FR 201. This road serves as a trailhead for many other trails. Unfortunately, the farther you travel, the more difficult it becomes; horse trailers are not recommended. It would be best to ride up FR 201 to the trail you want to ride.

WEST FORK TRAIL #260

Highlights: A short connector that connects the Thicket Spring Trail #95 to Cornucopia Trail #86.
Total Distance: 0.5 mile. Your ride can be lengthened via connecting trails.
Location: Mazatzal Wilderness
Type of Trail: Equestrian/Hiker
Connecting Trails: Thicket Spring Trail #95, Cornucopia Trail #86
Difficulty: Difficult
Elevation: 4,720 to 5,200 feet
Best Months: Year-round
Maps: Tonto National Forest, Mazatzal Wilderness
Special Considerations: Water is probably available at Thicket Springs.
Trailhead: No trailhead. Backcountry access via Cornucopia Trail #86 at the Peeley trailhead. From Mesa, travel north on AZ 87 about 46 miles to the Slate Creek Divide. Turn left on FR 201. This road serves as a trailhead for many other trails. Unfortunately, the farther you travel, the more difficult it becomes; horse trailers are not recommended. It would be best to ride up FR 201 to the trail you want to ride.

RED HILLS TRAIL #262

Highlights: A trail into very remote country. Some parts are steep and very difficult to follow.
Total Distance: 8.6 miles. Your ride can be lengthened via connecting trails.
Location: Mazatzal Wilderness
Type of Trail: Equestrian/Hiker

Connecting Trails: Mazatzal Divide Trail #23, Verde River Trail #11 (via Dutchman Grave Trail #22), Deadman Trail #25 (via Dutchman Grave Trail #22)
Difficulty: Difficult
Elevation: 2,820 to 6,280 feet
Best Months: Year-round
Maps: Tonto National Forest, Mazatzal Wilderness
Special Considerations: Recommended for experienced riders and horses. Water may be available at Fuller Seep.
Trailhead: No trailhead. Backcountry access via Mazatzal Divide Trail #23 at the City Creek trailhead. From Payson, drive west on Main Street (which becomes FR 406) approximately 11 miles. Turn right to the small parking area, which is about 100 yards beyond the steep switchback. This road is very steep and four-wheel-drive vehicles are needed for hauling horses and horse trailers. The Mazatzal Trail begins across the road from the trailhead.

WET BOTTOM TRAIL #269

Highlights: A little used trail that is very scenic and ends near the Bull Spring Cabin.
Total Distance: 9.4 miles. Your ride can be lengthened via connecting trails.
Location: Mazatzal Wilderness
Type of Trail: Equestrian/Hiker
Connecting Trails: Bull Spring Trail #34, Verde River Trail #11
Difficulty: Difficult
Elevation: 2,360 to 4,900 feet
Best Months: Year-round
Maps: Tonto National Forest, Mazatzal Wilderness
Special Considerations: Stock water is probably available on Bull Spring Trail #34.
Trailhead: No trailhead. Use the trailhead for Bull Spring Trail #34 or Verde River Trail #11. The latter requires fording the Verde River. See page 159 for Bull Spring Trail #34.

Globe Ranger District

UNA DEL OSO TRAIL #201

Highlights: A scenic connecting trail.
Total Distance: 0.3 mile. Your ride can be lengthened via connecting trails.
Location: Pinal Mountain Wilderness Recreation Area
Type of Trail: Equestrian/Hiker
Connecting Trails: Pioneer Pass Tollroad Trail #200
Difficulty: Easy
Elevation: 4,840 to 5,040 feet
Best Months: Spring and fall
Maps: Tonto National Forest, USGS: Pinal Peak
Trailhead: Access through the lower Six Shooter trailhead. From Globe, travel south on the Jess Hayes Road to Icehouse Canyon Road (FR 112). Turn south and go 6.6 miles to the bridge. Parking spaces are available on the left side of the road. The trail begins about 20 feet past the bridge.

MIDDLE TRAIL #202

Highlights: A connecting trail.
Total Distance: 0.6 mile. Your ride can be lengthened via connecting trials.
Location: Pinal Mountain Wilderness Recreation Area
Type of Trail: Equestrian/Hiker
Connecting Trails: Six Shooter Canyon Trail #197, Pineline Trail #193
Difficulty: Easy
Elevation: 7,640 to 7,760 feet
Best Months: Spring through fall
Maps: Tonto National Forest Service USGS: Pinal Peak
Special Considerations: No water is available.
Trailhead: From Globe, follow the Jess Hayes Road southeast to Icehouse Canyon Road (FR 112). Bear right and follow the Icehouse Canyon Road. At 2.5 miles, turn right on Kellner Canyon Road

(FR 55) and go about 5 miles to FR 651. Turn left and continue for about 10 miles. Stay left on FR 651 and proceed 0.3 mile to a small parking area east of the turnoff for the Fernell trailhead. The trail begins heading west, following the driveway of a burned-out summer home. The trail continues to proceed west and connects to Pineline Trail #193.

PIONEER PASS TOLLROAD TRAIL #200

Highlights: This trail was once a toll road and was built in 1883 as a route through the mountains to the Pioneer Mine.
Total Distance: 4.3 miles
Location: Pinal Mountain Wilderness Recreation Area
Type of Trail: Equestrian/Hiker
Connecting Trails: East Mountain Trail #214, Una Del Oso Trail #201, Check Dam Trail #190
Difficulty: Difficult
Elevation: 3,880 to 5,600 feet
Best Months: Spring through fall
Maps: Tonto National Forest USGS: Pinal Peak
Trailhead: From Globe, travel south on the Jess Hayes Road to the Icehouse Canyon Road and Six Shooter Canyon Road. Go left past the Globe Ranger District office. The road will bear left over the creek. Continue straight for about 2 miles to the trailhead. The trail starts off to the right, crossing the creek several times. You may park at the trailhead or at the wide turnouts along the creek.

KELLNER CANYON TRAIL #242

Highlights: A scenic trail that traverses several plant life zones.
Total Distance: 4.8 miles. Your ride can be lengthened via connecting trails.
Location: Pinal Mountain Wilderness Recreation Area
Type of Trail: Equestrian/Hiker
Connecting Trails: Icehouse Canyon Trail #198
Difficulty: Difficult
Elevation: 5,200 to 7,160 feet

Best Months: Spring and fall
Maps: Tonto National Forest USGS: Pinal Peak
Trailhead: Access is through the Kellner trailhead. From Globe, travel south on the Jess Hayes Road to the Icehouse Canyon Road (FR 112) and the Six Shooter Canyon Road (FR 222). Bear to the right on the Icehouse Canyon Road at about 2.5 miles. FR 112 will junction after the Kellner Canyon Road (FR 55). At this fork, bear right and continue on FR 55. At 0.6 mile, FR 55 meets FR 651. Turn left and drive about 9 miles farther to the trailhead. Cross the cattle guard. The trail begins on the left side of the road.

EAST MOUNTAIN TRAIL #214

Highlights: A scenic ride with panoramic views of Globe and Miami.
Total Distance: 4 miles. Your ride can be lengthened via connecting trails.
Location: Pinal Mountain Wilderness Recreation Area
Type of Trail: Equestrian/Hiker
Connecting Trails: Pioneer Pass Toll Road Trail #200
Difficulty: Difficult
Elevation: 5,560 to 6,156 feet
Best Months: Spring through fall
Maps: Tonto National Forest USGS: Pinal Peak
Trailhead: This trail has two access points. To reach the lower East Mountain trailhead, from Globe, travel southeast on the Jess Hayes Road to the Icehouse Canyon Road (FR 112). Turn right and continue past the Icehouse trailhead about 5 miles. The trail is on the left side of the road. To reach the Pioneer Pass trailhead, continue as above on FR 112 an additional mile to the trailhead. The Squaw Spring Trail begins on the west side of the road and East Mountain Trail #214 begins on the east side.

ICEHOUSE CANYON TRAIL #198

Highlights: Great views. Parts of this trail once served as a road to haul ice blocks to Glove and Miami. Some of these ice ponds can still be seen along the trail.

Total Distance: 4.5 miles. Your ride can be lengthened via connecting trails.

Location: Pinal Mountain Wilderness Recreation Area

Type of Trail: Equestrian/Hiker

Connecting Trails: Telephone Trail #192, Kellner Canyon Trail #242

Difficulty: Difficult

Elevation: 4,520 to 7,560 feet

Best Months: Spring through fall

Maps: Tonto National Forest USGS: Pinal Peak

Special Considerations: Hot in the summer.

Trailhead: From Globe, travel south on the Jess Hayes Road to the Icehouse Canyon Road (FR 112). Turn south and go about 5.5 miles. The trailhead is to the right, with parking spaces at the Icehouse CCC picnic area.

TELEPHONE TRAIL #192

Highlights: This trail passes by a turn-of-the-century sawmill.

Total Distance: 5 miles. Your ride can be lengthened via connecting trails.

Location: Pinal Mountain Wilderness Recreation Area

Type of Trail: Equestrian/Hiker

Connecting Trails: Icehouse Canyon Trail #198, Six Shooter Canyon Trail #197

Difficulty: Difficult

Elevation: 4,520 to 6,720 feet

Best Months: Spring and fall

Maps: Tonto National Forest USGS: Pinal Peak

Special Considerations: Hot in the summer.

Trailhead: There are two access points to this trail. From the north, access is via the Icehouse Recreation Area. From Globe, travel south on the Jess Hayes Road to the Icehouse Canyon Road (FR 112). Turn south and go 5.2 miles to the trailhead. Park at the picnic area. Or, from the south, use the Ferndell trailhead and connect via the Six Shooter Canyon Trail. From Globe, travel south on the Jess Hayes Road to the Icehouse Canyon Road

(FR 112). Turn south and go past the junction of FR 222. Bear right to Icehouse Canyon. Follow this road 2.5 miles to the junction of FR 55. Turn right. The pavement ends, but continue for 3 miles to FR 651. Turn left and go about 9 miles. Pass the cattle guards and the Kellner trailhead on FR 651. At the junction of FR 651C, follow FR 651 left toward the Upper Pinal Campground. Turn left toward Ferndell Springs. Trailhead parking is on the west-side drainage above the pump house.

SIX SHOOTER CANYON TRAIL #197

Highlights: Remains of old settlements, such as a sawmill, cabin, and old mineshaft. When the creek is flowing, there are several small waterfalls.

Total Distance: 6 miles. Your ride can be lengthened via connecting trails.

Location: Pinal Mountain Wilderness Recreation Area

Type of Trail: Equestrian/Hiker

Connecting Trails: Telephone Trail #192, Ferndell Trail #204, Middle Trail #202

Difficulty: Difficult

Elevation: 4,600 to 7,560 feet

Best Months: Early spring, fall, or winter

Maps: Tonto National Forest USGS: Pinal Peak

Special Considerations: Snowfields may exist.

Trailhead: Can be accessed from Icehouse Recreation Area, the lower Six Shooter trailhead, or the Ferndell trailhead. For the Icehouse Recreation Area, from Globe, travel south on the Jess Hayes Road to the Icehouse Canyon Road (FR 112). Turn south and go 5.5 miles. The trailhead is to the right with parking spaces at the Icehouse Picnic Area. For the lower Six Shooter trailhead proceed as above, but continue on FR 112 an additional 1.1 miles to the bridge. Parking spaces are available on the left side of the road. The trail begins about 20 feet past the bridge. To access the Ferndell trailhead, from Globe, travel south on the Jess Hayes Road to the Icehouse Canyon Road (FR 112). Turn and go past the junction of

FR 222. Bear right to Icehouse Canyon. Follow this road 2.5 miles to FR 55. Turn right. The pavement ends, but continue for 3 miles to FR 651. Turn left and follow FR 651 about 9 miles. Go past the cattle guard on FR 651. At the junction with FR 681, follow FR 651 left toward the Upper Pinal Campground. Turn left toward Fernell Springs. Trailhead parking is on the west-side drainage above the pump house.

PINELINE TRAIL #193

Highlights: This trail follows a pine covered ridge that offers spectacular views. A connecting trail that combines with Middle Trail #202 to lead out of the Pinal Mountains.

Total Distance: 0.8 mile. Your ride can be lengthened via connecting trails.

Location: Pinal Mountain Wilderness Recreation Area

Type of Trail: Equestrian/Hiker

Connecting Trails: Middle Trail #202, Bobtail Trail #194

Difficulty: Easy

Elevation: 7,560 to 7,640 feet

Best Months: Spring through fall

Maps: Tonto National Forest USGS: Pinal Peak

Trailhead: From Globe, travel southeast on the Jess Hayes Road, to the Icehouse Canyon Road (FR 112). Turn right and go 2.4 miles to the Kellner Canyon Road (FR 55). Turn right and travel 2.7 miles to FR 651. Turn left. Travel 11.4 miles to FR 651C. Turn right. Turn right on the Dead End Road. Travel 0.1 mile to a parking lot and a large FAA building. The trailhead is at the edge of the parking lot to the left of the building. Proceed on the Bobtail Ridge Trail for 0.5 miles; you will pass Mill Creek Trail #199.

FERNDELL TRAIL #204

Highlights: A connecting trail between the trails on the east end of the Pinal Mountains and those on the north side.

Total Distance: 0.8 mile. Your ride can be lengthened via connecting trails.

Location: Pinal Mountain Wilderness Recreation Area
Type of Trail: Equestrian/Hiker
Connecting Trails: Six Shooter Canyon Trail #197
Difficulty: Easy
Elevation: 7,520 to 7,800 feet
Best Months: Spring through fall
Maps: Tonto National Forest USGS: Pinal Peak
Trailhead: There are two points of access. For the Ferndell trailhead,
   from Globe, travel southeast on the Jess Hayes Road Follow the
   Icehouse Canyon Road (FR 112) to the right 2.4 miles to the Kellner
   Canyon Road (FR 55). Turn right and travel 2.7 miles to FR 651.
   Turn left and travel 11.4 miles to the junction with FR 651C. Follow
   FR 651 left toward Upper Pinal Campground. Turn left toward
   Ferndell Spring. Or, for the Pinal Peak trailhead, from Globe,
   travel southeast on the Jess Hayes Road. Follow the Icehouse
   Canyon Road (FR 112) to the right for 2.4 miles to the Kellner
   Canyon Road (FR 55). Turn right and travel 2.7 miles to FR 651.
   Turn left and travel 11.4 miles to the junction with FR 651C.
   Follow FR 651 to the right. The road will fork again. Stay to the
   right. At 0.1 mile is a three-way junction. Stay straight and go past
   the Squaw Spring trailhead to the parking area.

Mesa Ranger District

REAVIS RANCH TRAIL #109

Highlights: The northern section of this trail follows an old roadway to a former homestead; the southern portion traverses an old burn area.

Total Distance: 15.3 miles. Your ride can be lengthened via connecting trails.

Location: Superstition Mountain Wilderness

Type of Trail: Equestrian/Hiker

Connecting Trails: Reavis Gap Trail #117, Campaign Trail #256, West Pinto Trail #212, Roger's Canyon Trail #110 (via the Rogers Trough trailhead)

Difficulty: Moderate to difficult

Elevation: 3,620 to 5,360 feet

Best Months: Later fall through early spring

Maps: Tonto National Forest, Superstition Wilderness USGS: Mormon Flat Dam, Horse Mesa, Iron Mountain

Special Considerations: Very hot in the summer. No water is available.

Trailhead: From Phoenix, drive east on US 60 toward Apache Junction. At exit 196, drive north 1 mile on Idaho Road to AZ 88. Turn right and drive about 28 miles to the Reavis Ranch Road (FR 212). Turn right and follow the road to the trailhead. Saddle up and ride the last 3 miles to the trailhead, as this road is not recommended for horse trailers. This will allow access to Reavis Gap Trail #117 and the combined Campaign Trail #256 and Pinto Peak Trail #213.

BULL BASIN TRAIL #270

Highlights: An interesting trail to a basin area.

Total Distance: 4 miles

Location: Superstition Mountain Wilderness

Type of Trail: Equestrian/Hiker

Difficulty: Moderate

Elevation: 3,560 to 5,100 feet

Best Months: Late fall through spring

Maps: Tonto National Forest Service, Superstition Wilderness USGS: Mormon Flat Dam, Horse Mesa, Iron Mountain

Special Considerations: Very hot in the summer. No water is available.

Trailhead: From Superior, drive northeast on US 60 about 4 miles, past "Top of the World." Turn left on the paved Pinto Valley Mine Road (FR 287). FR 287 can be confusing through the mine area. Follow it for about 6.5 miles to the Mule Ranch Road (FR 287A). Turn off and park in this area. Ride the additional 5.6 miles to the trailhead.

DUTCHMAN'S TRAIL #104

Highlights: A lengthy trail with multiple connecting trails.

Total Distance: 18.2 miles. Your ride can be lengthened via connecting trails.

Location: Superstition Mountain Wilderness

Type of Trail: Equestrian/Hiker

Connecting Trails: Second Water Trail #236 (via First Water trailhead)

Difficulty: Moderate

Elevation: 2,280 to 3,250 feet

Best Months: Late fall through early spring

Maps: Tonto Forest Service, Superstition Wilderness USGS: Mormon Flat Dam, Horse Mesa, Iron Mountain

Special Considerations: Very hot in the summer. No water is available. Peralta Trail #102 and Bluff Springs Trail #235, which connect with this trail, are not recommended for horse travel.

Trailhead: There are two access points. For the Peralta trailhead, from Phoenix, travel east on US 60 about 8.5 miles and pass Apache Junction. At the Peralta Road (FR 77), turn right and proceed 8 miles to the trailhead. Parking is on the left inside the forest boundary and 0.1 mile prior to the main trailhead. For the First Water trailhead, from Phoenix, travel east on US 60 to exit 196. Drive north on Idaho Road for 1 mile to AZ 88. Turn right (north) and drive about 3.5 miles to Road 78, which is near milepost 200. Turn right and travel 3 miles to the parking area, which is on the left. Ride 0.5 mile to the main trailhead.

JF Trail #106

Highlights: A historic north-south trail named after a local rancher and cattleman.
Total Distance: 10.2 miles. Your ride can be lengthened via connecting trails.
Location: Superstition Mountain Wilderness
Type of Trail: Equestrian/Hiker
Connecting Trails: Woodbury Trail #114
Difficulty: Moderate
Elevation: 3,250 to 4,560 feet
Best Months: Late fall through early spring
Maps: Tonto National Forest, Superstition Wilderness USGS: Mormon Flat Dam, Horse Mesa, Iron Mountain
Special Considerations: Very hot in the summer. No water is available.
Trailhead: From Phoenix, drive east on US 60 toward Apache Junction. Get off at exit 196. Drive 1 mile north on Idaho Road to AZ 88. Turn left and drive about 22 miles to the Tortilla Road (FR 213). Turn off at the trailhead. The road ends in 2 miles. There is a corral with additional parking a short distance up the road.

Peter's Trail #105

Highlights: Scenic views
Total Distance: 7 miles. You can lengthen your ride via connecting trails.
Location: Superstition Mountain Wilderness
Type of Trail: Equestrian/Hiker
Connecting Trails: Dutchman's Trail #104, JF Trail #106
Difficulty: Moderate
Elevation: 3,100 to 3,800 feet
Best Months: Late fall through early spring
Maps: Tonto National Forest, Superstition Wilderness USGS: Mormon Flat Dam, Horse Mesa, Iron Mountain
Special Considerations: Very hot in the summer. No water is available. Parts of the trail may be vague and very hard to find.

Trailhead: From Phoenix, drive east on US 60 toward Apache Junction. Get off at Exit 196. Drive 1 mile north on Idaho Road to AZ 88. Turn left and drive about 22 miles to the Tortilla Road (FR 213). Turn off at the trailhead. The road ends in 2 miles. There is a corral with additional parking a short distance up the road.

CAMPAIGN TRAIL #256

Highlights: A scenic, little-used trail that parallels Campaign Creek and travels to Haunted Mountain through remote wilderness.
Total Distance: 5.7 miles. Your ride can be lengthened via connecting trails.
Location: Superstition Wilderness
Type of Trail: Equestrian/Hiker
Connecting Trails: West Pinto Trail #212, Reavis Gap Trail #117
Difficulty: Moderate
Elevation: 2,400 to 4,040 feet
Best Months: Year-round
Maps: Tonto National Forest, Superstition Wilderness
Special Considerations: Very hot in the summer. This trail has been reconstructed using the old Pinto Peak Trail. It is equestrian-friendly, though not all connecting trails may be.
Trailhead: There are two trailhead access points. For southern access, use the Miles trailhead. From Superior, drive northwest on US 60 about 4 miles past "Top of the World." Turn left on the paved Pinto Valley Mine Road (FR 287) just east of the Pinto Creek Bridge. This road goes through a mining area and can be confusing. Follow FR 287 for about 6.5 miles to the Miles Ranch Road (FR 287A). Park here and saddle up. Ride the 5.6 miles to the trailhead. The northern access is the Campaign trailhead, which requires four-wheel-drive and smaller horse trailers. From the junction of AZ 88 and US 60, drive north on AZ 88 21.2 miles to Cross P Ranch Road (FR 449). Turn left and drive about 2 miles to FR 449A. Turn left and drive about 8 miles to the trailhead. The road is rough, so you may want to unload your horses and ride to the trailhead.

TWO BAR RIDGE TRAIL #119

Highlights: A very scenic trail in a remote portion of the Superstition Mountains.

Total Distance: 8.3 miles. Your ride can be lengthened via connecting trails.

Location: Superstition Mountain Wilderness

Type of Trail: Equestrian/Hiker

Connecting Trails: Reavis Gap Trail #117, Reavis Ranch Trail #109 (via Reavis Gap Trail #117)

Difficulty: Difficult

Elevation: 4,200 to 4,900 feet

Best Months: Late fall through early spring

Maps: Tonto National Forest, Superstition Wilderness USGS: Piñon Mountain, Two Bar Mountain

Special Considerations: Very hot in the summer. Some portions of this trail are rocky and overgrown, and may be hard to follow.

Trailhead: Use the Tule trailhead. From Phoenix, drive east on US 60 about 8.5 miles past Apache Junction and get off at exit 196. Drive north 1 mile on the Idaho Road to AZ 88. Turn right and drive about 3.5 miles north to Road 78 (milepost 200). Turn right and follow Road 78 for 3 miles. Horse trailer parking is on the left, 0.5 mile prior to the main trailhead.

LOST GOLDMINE TRAIL

Highlights: Since this book has limited horse trails in the Superstition Mountain area, I have taken the liberty to include the Lost Goldmine Trail. The trails are not at the altitude of the other trails mentioned in this book, but I thought you might enjoy them. The trails are part of the Superstition Land Trust Area on perpetual lease from the Arizona State Land Department.

Total Distance: 11.5 miles

Location: Superstition Mountains

Type of Trail: Equestrian/Hiker

Connecting Trails: Jacob's Crosscut Trail

Difficulty: Easy to moderate

Best Months: November through March.

Maps: Lost Goldmine Trail Map, USGS: Goldfield

Special Considerations: Very hot in the summer. For additional information, contact Superstition Area Land Trust, 480-983-2345.

Trailhead: For the north trailhead, from Phoenix, travel east on US 60 to Apache Junction and get off at exit 204 (Peralta Road). Travel north about 7 miles. At the "Y," stay to the left. Proceed about 1 mile and turn left into the large parking lot. This lot, which is the best trailhead for horse trailers, is prior to the entry to the Tonto National Forest. Or, from Phoenix, travel east on US 60 to mile marker 203, Kings Ranch Road, which goes through the hamlet of Gold Canyon. Turn left at the Walgreen's (third light). This is Kings Ranch Road. Continue for 3 miles to Baseline Road. After the cattle guard, turn right and follow the meandering paved road to the "T" at the stop sign. Turn right on Cloud View. Go to the end of the road, about 1 mile, to the parking lot. The parking lot is small, but is being enlarged.

BALLANTINE TRAIL #283

Highlights: Splendid views, interesting rock formations, and a desert riparian area.

Total Distance: 10 miles. Your ride can be lengthened via connecting trails.

Location: Four Peaks Wilderness

Type of Trail: Equestrian/Hiker

Connecting Trails: Pine Creek Loop Trail #280

Difficulty: Difficult

Elevation: 2,520 to 4,200 feet

Best Months: Year-round

Maps: Tonto National Forest USGS: Mine Mountain, Boulder Mountain

Special Considerations: The trail may appear vague and difficult to find as it approaches the east side of Pine Mountain.

Trailhead: There are two access points. From the north, from Payson, travel south on AZ 87 28 miles. The trailhead is on the east side of the highway. Or, from Mesa, travel north on AZ 87 about 38 miles to FR 143. Proceed east on FR 143 to the Cline trailhead.

SOLDIER CAMP TRAIL #83

Highlights: Panoramic views. Transition from desert to forested mountain. The southern half of the trail is an old Jeep road.
Total Distance: 8 miles. Your ride can be lengthened via connecting trails.
Location: Four Peaks Wilderness
Type of Trail: Equestrian/Hiker
Connecting Trails: Lower Soldier Camp Trail #84, Cane Spring Trail #77
Difficulty: Difficult
Elevation: 3,320 to 5,450 feet
Best Months: Year-round
Maps: Tonto National Forest
Special Considerations: Very hot in the summer.
Trailhead: From Mesa, drive north on AZ 87 to about 11.5 miles north of the Verde River Bridge (just past the Desert Vista Rest Stop). Turn right (east) on the Four Peaks Road (FR 143) and drive 16 miles to the trailhead.

FOUR PEAKS TRAIL #130

Highlights: Traverses the northern and eastern flanks of the Four Peaks along Buckhorn Ridge.
Total Distance: 10 miles. Your ride can be lengthened via connecting trails.
Location: Four Peaks Wilderness
Type of Trail: Equestrian/Hiker
Connecting Trails: Amethyst Trail #253, Oak Flat Trail #123, Alder Creek Trail #82, Brown's Trail #133
Difficulty: Easy to difficult
Elevation: 3,800 to 6,600 feet
Best Months: Year-round
Maps: Tonto National Forest
Special Considerations: Very hot in the summer. The trail is steep and may be difficult to find in the eastern and southern sections and along the Buckhorn Ridge.

Trailhead: From Mesa, drive north on AZ 87 to about 11.5 miles north of the Verde River Bridge (just past the Desert Vista Rest Stop). Turn right (east) on the Four Peaks Road (FR 143). Continue 18.8 miles to the El Oso Divide. At this point, make a sharp right (south) onto FR 648. Park here, as the road ahead is not suitable for horse trailers. Ride 1.3 miles to the trailhead. Or, From Punkin Center, drive south on AZ 188. Turn right on FR 143 and drive 9 miles to the El Oso Divide. The road will turn south and go along the ridge top. Park at the junction with FR 648 and ride 1.3 miles to the trailhead. Or, from Roosevelt Dam, drive northwest on AZ 188 3.4 miles to FR 429. Turn left and drive about 6 miles to the trailhead (a four-wheel-drive road).

BROWN'S TRAIL #133

Highlights: A connecting spur trail that connects to Amethyst Trail #253.
Total Distance: 2 miles. Your ride can be lengthened via connecting trails.
Location: Four Peaks Wilderness
Type of Trail: Equestrian/Hiker
Connecting Trails: Four Peaks Trail #130, Amethyst Trail #253
Difficulty: Difficult
Elevation: 5,700 to 6,700 feet
Best Months: Year-round
Maps: Tonto National Forest
Special Considerations: Water is not available.
Trailhead: From Mesa, drive north on AZ 87 to about 11.5 miles north of the Verde River Bridge (just past the Desert Vista Rest Stop). Turn right (east) onto the Four Peaks Road (FR 143). Continue 18.8 miles to the El Oso Divide. At this point, make a sharp right (south) onto FR 648. Park here, as the road ahead is not suitable for horse trailers. Ride 1.3 miles to the trailhead. Or, from Punkin Center, drive south on AZ 188. Turn right onto FR 143 and drive 9 miles to the El Oso Divide. The road will turn south and go along the ridge top. Park at the junction with FR 648 and ride 1.3 miles to the trailhead. Or, from Roosevelt Dam, drive northwest on AZ 188 3.4 miles to

FR 429. Turn left and drive about 6 miles to the trailhead (a four-wheel-drive road).

AMETHYST TRAIL #253

Highlights: This trail ends at the privately owned Amethyst Mine.
Total Distance: 3 miles. Your ride can be lengthened via connecting trails.
Location: Four Peaks Wilderness
Type of Trail: Equestrian/Hiker
Connecting Trails: Brown's Trail #133, Four Peaks Trail #130
Difficulty: Difficult
Elevation: 5,800 to 6,800 feet
Best Months: Year-round
Maps: Tonto National Forest
Special Considerations: The trail is narrow along the western flank of the Four Peaks. Experienced trail horses and experienced riders are recommended. Do not enter the mine property without prior written permission.
Trailhead: Backcountry access is obtained by way of Lone Pine Saddle trailhead and connecting to Brown's Trail #133. From Mesa, drive north on AZ 87 to about 11.5 miles north of the Verde River Bridge (just past the Desert Vista Rest Stop). Turn right (east) onto the Four Peaks Road (FR 143). Continue 18.8 miles to the El Oso Divide. At this point, make a sharp right (south) onto FR 648. Park here, as the road ahead is not suitable for horse trailers. Ride 1.3 miles to the trailhead. Or, from Punkin Center, drive south on AZ 188. Turn right onto FR 143 and drive 9 miles to the El Oso Divide. The road will turn south and go along the ridge top. Park at the junction with FR 648 and ride 1.3 miles to the trailhead. Or, from Roosevelt Dam, drive northwest on AZ 188 3.4 miles to FR 429. Turn left and drive about 6 miles to the trailhead (a four-wheel-drive road).

Payson Ranger District

FOSSIL SPRINGS TRAIL #18

Highlights: A pretty trail that was featured in *Arizona Highways* magazine, and was once a wagon trail. There is a swimming hole at the end of the trail.
Total Distance: 3.1 miles
Location: Fossil Springs Wilderness
Type of Trail: Equestrian/Hiker
Difficulty: Difficult
Elevation: 4,320 to 5,600 feet
Best Months: Year-round
Maps: Tonto National Forest USGS: Strawberry
Special Considerations: Can be hot in the summer.
Trailhead: From Strawberry and the intersection near the Strawberry Lodge, travel west on FR 428, which becomes FR 708. Continue about 4 miles to the trailhead on the right.

OAK SPRING TRAIL #16

Highlights: A segment of the Arizona Trail.
Total Distance: 5 miles
Location: Pine
Type of Trail: Equestrian/Hiker
Difficulty: Easy to Moderate
Elevation: 5,320 to 5,700 feet
Best Months: Year-round
Maps: Tonto National Forest USGS: Pine and Buckhead Mesa
Special Considerations: This trail crosses AZ 87, so use extreme caution. A portion of this trail is FR 428.
Trailhead: From Payson, travel north on AZ 87 about 13 miles. The Pine trailhead is on the right, about 1 mile from the village of Pine.

HIGHLINE TRAIL #31

Highlights: This National Recreation Trail was established in 1870. Author Zane Grey once lived in this area; his camp was destroyed in the 1990 Dude Fire.

Total Distance: 50.2 miles. Your ride can be altered via connecting trails.

Location: Mogollon Rim

Type of Trail: Equestrian/Hiker

Connecting Trails: Babe Haught Trail #143, Col. Devin Trail #290, Derrick Trail #33, Donahue Trail #27, Drew Trail #291, Geronimo Trail #240, Horton Creek Trail #285, Myrtle Trail #30, Promontory Trail #278, Pump Station Trail #296, Red Rock Trail #294, See Canyon Trail #184

Difficulty: Difficult

Elevation: 5,360 to 6,620 feet

Best Months: Year-round

Maps: Tonto National Forest USGS: Buckhead Mesa, Pine, Kehl Diamond Point, Promontory Butte, Woods Canyon

Trailhead: There are multiple access points. Consult the Tonto National Forest map for trailhead's at Pine, Redrock, Geronimo, Washington Park Hatchery, See Canyon Trail #184 (see below), and Two Sixty.

See Canyon Trail #184

Highlights: A beautiful trail in the fall with great colors from the hardwoods and aspen trees.

Total Distance: 3.5 miles

Location: Mogollon Rim

Type of Trail: Equestrian/Hiker

Connecting Trails: Highline Trail #31

Difficulty: Difficult

Elevation: 6,100 to 7,860 feet

Best Months: Year-round

Maps: Tonto National Forest USGS: Promontory Butte

Special Considerations: Water may be found in the first two miles, but beware—this is not for human consumption. The trail crosses Christopher Creek and has the potential to flood. Snowfields may exist in the winter.

Trailhead: From Payson, drive east on AZ 260 to Christopher Creek. Turn left to the trailhead, which is west of Christopher Creek and almost across from the Christopher Creek Store.

Pleasant Valley Ranger District

DEEP CREEK TRAIL #128

Highlights: An access trail to the Sierra Ancha Wilderness.

Total Distance: 5 miles. Your ride can be lengthened via connecting trails.

Location: Sierra Ancha Wilderness

Type of Trail: Equestrian/Hiker

Connecting Trails: Coon Spring Trail #124

Difficulty: Easy

Elevation: 5,000 to 5,500 feet

Best Months: Year-round

Maps: Tonto National Forest USGS: Aztec Park

Special Considerations: There is limited water access.

Trailhead: From Claypool (between Miami and Globe), travel northwest on AZ 88 about 15 miles to AZ 288. Turn right (north) and go 6.6 miles to the Cherry Creek Road (FR 203). Turn east and go 9 miles, then turn north on FR 203A. Drive about 6.5 miles to the trailhead.

PARKER CREEK TRAIL #160

Highlights: A pleasant, scenic connecting trail.

Total Distance: 3.4 miles. Your ride can be lengthened via connecting trails.

Location: Sierra Ancha Wilderness

Type of Trail: Equestrian/Hiker

Connecting Trails: Coon Creek Trail #254, Rim Trail #139

Difficulty: Difficult

Elevation: 5,100 to 7,000 feet

Best Months: Spring through fall

Maps: Tonto National Forest: USGS Aztec Peak

Special Considerations: AZ 487 is closed December 15 through March 30. Many of the trail passages are narrow and steeply sloped. For experienced riders and trail horses only.

Trailhead: From Claypool (between Miami and Globe), drive north-west on AZ 88 about 15 miles to AZ 288. Turn right and drive north about 20 miles to the former Sierra Ancha Experimental Station. Turn right into the graveled parking area just outside the facility gate. Ride 100 yards to the trail, signed on the left near the flagpole.

LUCKY STRIKE TRAIL #144

Highlights: A great horse trail.
Total Distance: 5 miles. Your ride can be lengthened via connecting trails.
Location: Sierra Ancha Wilderness
Type of Trail: Equestrian/Hiker
Connecting Trails: Center Mountain Trail #142, Grapevine Trail #135
Difficulty: Difficult
Elevation: 4,000 to 6,800 feet
Best Months: Spring through fall
Maps: Tonto National Forest USGS: Aztec Peak
Trailhead: From Claypool (between Miami and Globe), travel north-west on AZ 88 about 15 miles to AZ 288. Turn right and drive north 27.5 miles. Just past Reynold's Creek, turn right (east) on FR 410. Drive about 2.5 miles to FR 235. You will need a four-wheel-drive at this point. Turn left and travel 2.5 miles to the trailhead.

CENTER MOUNTAIN #142

Highlights: A scenic connecting trail.
Total Distance: 2.5 miles. Your ride can be lengthened via connecting trails.
Location: Sierra Ancha Wilderness
Type of Trail: Equestrian/Hiker
Connecting Trails: Lucky Strike Trail #144
Difficulty: Difficult
Elevation: 6,700 to 7,500 feet

Best Months: Spring through fall
Maps: Tonto National Forest USGS: Aztec Peak
Trailhead: From Claypool (between Miami and Globe), travel north-west on AZ 88 about 15 miles to AZ 288. Turn right and drive north 27.5 miles. Just past Reynold's Creek, turn right (east) on FR 410. Drive about 2.5 miles to FR 235. You will need a four-wheel-drive at this point. Turn left and travel 2.5 miles to the trailhead.

GRAPEVINE TRAIL #135

Highlights: A pleasant and easy ride, particularly when connecting with Lucky Strike Trail #144. Overlooks Cherry Creek.
Total Distance: 5 miles. Your ride can be lengthened via a connecting trail.
Location: Sierra Ancha Wilderness
Type of Trail: Equestrian/Hiker
Connecting Trails: Lucky Strike Trail #144
Difficulty: Easy
Elevation: 4,400 to 4,900 feet
Best Months: Spring through fall
Maps: Tonto National Forest USGS: Aztec Peak
Trailhead: From Claypool (between Miami and Globe), travel north-west on AZ 88 about 15 miles to AZ 288. Turn right and drive north 6.6 miles to the Cherry Creek Road (FR 203). Go east 31.8 miles to the trailhead.

COON SPRING TRAIL #124

Highlights: Indian ruins at Oak Creek Cabin.
Total Distance: 4 miles. Your ride can be lengthened via connecting trails.
Location: Sierra Ancha Wilderness
Type of Trail: Equestrian/Hiker
Connecting Trails: Deep Creek Trail #128, Coon Creek Trail #254
Difficulty: Easy
Elevation: 4,400 to 5,100 feet
Best Months: Year-round
Maps: Tonto National Forest USGS: Aztec Peak

Special Considerations: Very hot in the summer. Water is not available.

Trailhead: There are two access points. From Claypool (between Miami and Globe), travel northwest on AZ 88 about 15 miles to AZ 288. Turn right and go north 6.6 miles to the Cherry Creek Road (FR 203). Go east 9 miles. Turn north on FR 203A and go about 6.5 miles to the trailhead. Or, from Claypool (between Miami and Globe), travel northeast on AZ 88 about 15 miles to AZ 288. Turn right and drive north about 15 miles to FR 189. Turn right and go east 5 miles to the Oak Creek Cabin and the trailhead.

COON CREEK TRAIL #254

Highlights: Great views.

Total Distance: 4.4 miles. Your ride can be lengthened via connecting trails.

Location: Sierra Ancha Wilderness

Type of Trail: Equestrian/Hiker

Connecting Trails: Coon Spring Trail #124, Parker Creek Trail #160

Difficulty: Difficult

Elevation: 4,700 to 7,100 feet

Best Months: Spring through fall

Maps: Tonto National Forest USGS: Aztec Peak

Special Considerations: No water is available.

Trailhead: There are two access points. From Claypool (between Miami and Globe), travel northwest on AZ 88 about 15 miles to AZ 288. Turn right and go north 6.6 miles to the Cherry Creek Road (FR 203). Go east 9 miles, then turn north on FR 203A. Follow FR 203A about 6.5 miles to the trailhead. Or, from Claypool (between Miami and Globe), travel northeast on AZ 88 about 15 miles to AZ 288. Turn right and drive north about 15 miles to FR 189. Turn right and go east 5 miles to the Oak Creek Cabin and the trailhead.

RIM TRAIL #139

Highlights: A scenic ride.

Total Distance: 7.6 miles. Your ride can be lengthened via connecting trails.

Location: Sierra Ancha Wilderness
Type of Trail: Equestrian/Hiker
Connecting Trails: Parker Creek #160, Murphy Trail #141, Moody Point Trail #140, Coon Spring Trail #124
Difficulty: Easy
Elevation: 6,400 to 6,800 feet
Best Months: Spring through fall
Maps: Tonto National Forest USGS: Aztec Peak
Special Considerations: FR 487 is closed December 15 through March 30.
Trailhead: From Claypool (between Miami and Globe) travel northwest on AZ 88 about 15 miles to AZ 288. Turn right and go 25.5 miles to the Workman Creek Road (FR 487). Turn right and go east 5.5 miles to the Carr trailhead. Rim Trail #139 begins 1 mile down from Parker Creek Trail #160. Or, continue farther on FR 487 to the Moody Point trailhead. Rim Trail #139 begins about 1 mile down Moody Point Trail #140. Or, continue farther on FR 487 to the Murphy trailhead. Rim Trail #139 begins about 1 mile down Coon Springs Trail #124.

MOODY POINT TRAIL #140

Highlights: One of the longest, most difficult trails in the Sierra Ancha Wilderness Area. Prehistoric ruins along the trail. A beaver pond on Cherry Creek.
Total Distance: 9.5 miles
Location: Sierra Ancha Wilderness
Type of Trail: Equestrian/Hiker
Difficulty: Difficult
Elevation: 3,000 to 7,200 feet
Best Months: Spring through fall
Maps: Tonto National Forest USGS: Aztec Peak
Special Considerations: FR 487 is closed December 15 to March 30. For experienced riders and trail horses only.
Trailhead: There are two access points. From Claypool, take AZ 288 and drive north about 25.5 miles to FR 487, which is just past the

Workman's Creek Bridge. You will probably need a four-wheel drive at this point. Go east on FR 487 about 6 miles to the trailhead. Or, from Claypool drive north on AZ 288 6.6 miles to the Cherry Creek Road (FR 203). Go east 18.8 miles to the trailhead and the small parking area.

MCFADDEN HORSE TRAIL #146

Highlights: A dead-end trail to the pine-covered McFadden Horse Mountain with scenic views.
Total Distance: 6 miles
Location: Sierra Ancha Wilderness
Type of Trail: Equestrian/Hiker
Difficulty: Moderate
Elevation: 5,600 to 7,400 feet
Best Months: Spring through fall
Maps: Tonto National Forest USGS: Aztec Peak
Trailhead: From Claypool (between Miami and Globe), travel northwest on AZ 88 about 15 miles to AZ 288. Turn right and drive north about 27.5 miles (just past Reynolds Creek). Turn right (east) on FR 410. Drive 2.5 miles to FR 235. You probably will need a four-wheel-drive at this point. Turn left and drive 0.5 mile to the trailhead.

BEAR FLAT TRAIL #178

Highlights: A pleasant beautiful ride that is occasionally steep.
Total Distance: 9.25 miles
Location: Hellsgate Wilderness
Type of Trail: Equestrian/Hiker
Difficulty: Difficult
Elevation: 5,200 to 5,800 feet
Best Months: Year-round
Maps: Tonto National Forest
Special Considerations: FR 405 is steep and two-wheel-drive vehicles with horse trailers are not recommended.

Trailhead: From Payson, go east on AZ 260 11.4 miles. Turn south on FR 405A and go 2.7 miles to FR 405. Continue south on FR 405 for 3.2 miles. The trail begins across the creek near the private land.

BOYER TRAIL #148

Highlights: Scenic views. Prehistoric ruins and the Boyer Cabin. This trail follows Boyer Creek and bluffs above Salome Creek and eventually joins Hell's Hole Trail #284.

Total Distance: 5 miles. Your ride can be lengthened via connecting trails.

Location: Salome Wilderness

Type of Trail: Equestrian/Hiker

Connecting Trails: Hell's Hole Trail #284

Difficulty: Moderate

Elevation: 4,080 to 6,000 feet

Best Months: Year-round

Maps: Tonto National Forest USGS: Armer Mountain

Special Considerations: There is probably water at Hopkins Spring. The trail may be overgrown and difficult to follow in some places. Do not proceed very far on the Hell's Hole Trail, as it can be dangerous for horses. Snowfields may be encountered in winter.

Trailhead: From Claypool (between Miami and Globe), travel northwest on AZ 88 about 15 miles to AZ 288. Go north for 27.5 miles. Just beyond Reynold's Creek, turn right (east) on FR 410. Drive about 4 miles to the Reynold's trailhead. Take this trail to connect to Boyer Trail #148. If you have a four-wheel-drive, you can access the trailhead by traveling north from Roosevelt Lake on AZ 288. Take FDR 60 west about 9 miles. Turn north on FDR 895 and go 12 miles to the Boyer Cabin and the trailhead.

CIENEGA TRAIL #145

Highlights: Ruins of an old mining facility.

Total Distance: 3.3 miles. Your ride can be lengthened via connecting trails.

Location: Sierra Ancha Wilderness

Type of Trail: Equestrian/Hiker
Connecting Trails: McFadden Horse Trail #146
Difficulty: Moderate
Elevation: 5,678 to 5,841 feet
Best Months: Year-round
Maps: Tonto National Forest USGS: Aztec Peak
Special Considerations: Snow fields may exist during the winter.
Trailhead: From Claypool (between Miami and Globe), travel north
on AZ 88 about 15 miles to AZ 288. Turn right and travel north
28 miles to Reynold's Creek Road (FR 410). Turn right and drive
2.5 miles to FR 235. You will now need four-wheel-drive. Turn left
and drive about 0.5 mile to the trailhead.

Appendix

Horse Camps

THE NATIONAL FORESTS IN ARIZONA are equestrian-friendly, and, aside from offering great riding trails, include camping areas and "horse camps." The latter areas designed for horse trailer parking and camping, usually have corrals. Please clean up and rake out the area upon your departure.

The camping fees listed below are always subject to change. Call the pertinent ranger district prior to your departure for up-to-date information about the camp(s) you wish to use.

Apache-Sitgreaves National Forest

KP Cienaga Campground, Alpine Ranger District
Facilities: Drinking water. Outhouses. Picnic tables. Grills. Fire pits. The corral is within 50 yards of the campground.
Fees: None
Season: Spring through fall
Elevation: 9,000 feet
Directions: From Alpine, travel southwest on US 191. Turn left on FR 155 and go toward Hannagan Meadow and the campground.
Contact: Alpine Ranger District, 928-339-4384

Strayhorse Campground, Clifton Ranger District
Facilities: Drinking water. Vault toilets. Picnic tables. Grills and fire pits. Corrals.
Fees: None
Season: Spring through fall

Elevation: 7,600 feet

Directions: From Alpine, travel south on US 666 26 miles to the campground.

Trails: Two horse trails lead out of the campground. Raspberry Trail #35 (see page 6) heads toward the Blue Range Primitive Area. The second trail goes west of Highland Trail toward the San Carlos Indian Reservation, following the base of the Mogollon Rim.

Contact: Clifton Ranger District, 928-687-1301

Los Burros Campground (primitive), Lakeside Ranger District

Facilities: Drinking water (from a spring); water needs to be purified for human consumption. Picnic tables. Fire rings. No toilets. Corrals are located 50 yards from the campsite. Other primitive areas suitable for horse camping are Danstone Spring, and Brown Spring, both located in the vicinity of the Los Burros Campground.

Fees: None

Season: May through October

Elevation: 7,820 feet

Directions: From Lakeside, travel east on AZ 260 to McNary. Turn left on FR 224 toward Vernon and continue to the campground.

Trails: Blue Ridge Trail #107 (see page 41) and Los Burros Trail #631 (see page 43) lead out of the Los Burros Campground.

Contact: Lakeside Ranger District, 928-368-5111

Lakeside Campground (operated by the Forest Service)

Facilities: Picnic tables. Fire rings. Toilets. Drinking water. Grills. No corrals, but a private stable is located behind the campground.

Fees: $5 per day

Season: May through October

Elevation: 7,000 feet

Directions: From Lakeside, drive northwest on AZ 260 about 0.5 mile. The campground is in the middle of town, across from the ranger district office.

Contact: Lakeside Ranger District 928-368-5111

Gabaldon Campground (horse camping only), Springerville Ranger District

Facilities: Portable toilets. Corrals. Water horses in the creek. This campground can accommodate up to five parties with three or four horses each. Because of the access road, a trailer no longer than 16 feet is recommended.

Fees: None

Season: Spring through fall

Elevation: 8,500 feet

Directions: From Pinetop-Lakeside, take AZ 260 east to McNary. Continue on AZ 260 to the Sunrise turnoff (FR 273). Turn right and travel about 10 miles to the campground.

Contact: Springerville Ranger District, 928-333-4372

Coconino National Forest

Little Elden Springs Horse Camp, Peaks Ranger District

Facilities: Pull-through campsites. Picnic tables. Restrooms. Water. Hitching rails. Dumpsters.

Fees: $10 per night, reservation fee

Season: May 1 through September 30

Elevation: 7,200 feet

Directions: From Flagstaff, travel northeast on US 89 to FR 556. Turn left and drive 2 miles to FR 556A. Turn right (north), and continue to the campground.

Trails: A trail leading out of the campground connects to a network of riding trails in the Mt. Elden/Dry Lake Hills Trail System.

Contact: Peaks Ranger District, 928-526-0866

Coronado National Forest

Price Canyon Ranch (privately owned), Douglas Ranger District

Facilities: Privately owned ranch adjacent to Forest Service land. Horse stables available.

Contact: Stan and Pat Smith, 520-558-2383

Ramsey Vista Campground, Sierra Vista Ranger District

Facilities: Picnic tables. Fire rings. Tent pads. Toilets. Garbage bins. Horse corrals nearby. Horses are not allowed in the campground proper.

Fees: $5 per night, $3 for day use

Season: Year-round, but ranger district may be closed in the winter depending on weather

Elevation: 7,200 feet

Directions: From Tucson, drive east on I-10 to AZ 90 (exit 302). Drive south 25 miles to Sierra Vista. At 8 miles south of Sierra Vista, AZ 90 turns west on the Carr Canyon Road (FR 368). Travel 7 miles to the road terminus and the campground.

Trails: Carr Trail #107, Comfort Springs Trail #109 (both connect to Crest Trail #103 [see page 88], which connects with multiple trails)

Contact: Sierra Vista Ranger District, 520-378-0801

Cunningham Camp and Public Corral, Safford Ranger District

Facilities: Undeveloped campsites in a stand of aspen and Douglas fir. No water. Free waste station in the Ivanhoe Manufactured Home Sales lot on US 70/191 in Safford.

Fees: None

Season: May 16 through November 14, depending on weather

Elevation: 9,000 feet

Directions: From Safford, travel south on US 191 6 miles to AZ 366. Turn right and go 26 miles to the campground. (Although paved and well maintained, AZ 366 is steep and curvy with switchbacks.)

Trails: Grant Hill Loop Trail #322, Cunningham Loop Trail #316, Grant Creek Trail #305 (see page 91).

Contact: Safford Ranger District, 928-428-4150

Kaibab National Forest

Kaibab has multiple areas conducive to horse camping, but none specifically designed or denoted as horse camps. Contact the ranger district in which you plan to ride for suggestions on camping with your horse.

Prescott National Forest

Groom Creek Horse Camp, Bradshaw Ranger District
Facilities: Three loops, A through C, with hitching posts at each site. Water trough on each loop. Sites are spacious among a mixture of oak and ponderosa pine. Only campers with horses are permitted in the campground.
Fees: $10 per day
Season: May 1 through October 31
Elevation: 6,000 feet
Directions: In Prescott, at the intersection of Gurley Road and Mt. Vernon Avenue, turn south on South Mt. Vernon Avenue, which becomes the Senator Highway. Continue on the Senator Highway for 5.7 miles to the campground sign. Turn right into the campground.
Trails: Groom Creek Loop #307 (see page 137), Inter Loop Trail #383
Contact: Bradshaw Ranger District, 928-443-8000

Tonto National Forest

Pioneer Pass, Globe Ranger District
Facilities: A primitive campground near the pass offers access to the Mazatzal Wilderness. Water horses from the Verde River. Water is provided into the campground only from Memorial Day through October 15 because of snow. Designated horse use area with hitching rails, campsites, and enough parking for horse trailers.
Fees: None
Season: Year-round

Elevation: 6,000 feet

Directions: In Globe, from US 60, turn left at the sign to the Globe Ranger Station. Continue for 1.6 miles, following the signs to the Globe Ranger Station to Icehouse Canyon Road. Bear right onto Icehouse Canyon Road and go 1.8 miles to the stop sign (FR 112 and FR 55 and Kellner Canyon Road). Continue straight onto FR 112 and go 7 miles to the campground. Two miles past the stop sign, FR 112 becomes a winding, single-lane dirt road, signs of severe winter erosion and deep rutting. The road is rough and not trailer-friendly.

Trails: East Mountain Trail #214 (see page 170)

Contact: Globe Ranger District. 928-402-6200

Houston Mesa Horse Camp, Payson Ranger District

Facilities: Restrooms. Showers. Corrals. Tables. Grills. Water.

Fees: $10 per night

Season: Year-round

Elevation: 5,200 feet

Directions: From Payson, travel north on AZ 87 2 miles to the junction of Houston Mesa Road (FR 199). Turn east and drive 0.25 mile to the campground.

Trails: Leading out of the campground are the 6-mile Houston Mesa Trail, which consists of two loop trails, the Shoofly Loop (4 miles) and the Houston Loop (3.7 miles). The ride is easy, with good views of the Mogollon Rim. The trail traverses juniper and piñon woodlands to access the Shoofly Village ruins.

Contact: Payson Ranger District, 928-474-7900

Trail Index